24 TIMELESS TAKES ON THE WORLD'S
MOST POPULAR SWEATER

MY FAVORITE CARDIGANS TO KNIT

BIRGITTA FORSLUND

PHOTOGRAPHY ÅSA DAHLGREN

TRAFALGAR SQUARE
North Pomfret, Vermont

First published in the United States of America
in 2014 by
Trafalgar Square Books
North Pomfret, Vermont 05053

© Birgitta Forslund, 2013
First published by Bonnier Fakta, Stockholm, Sweden

The instructions and material lists in this book were carefully reviewed by
the author and editor; however, accuracy cannot be guaranteed. The author
and publisher cannot be held liable for errors.

ISBN: 978-1-57076-662-6

Library of Congress Control Number: 2014943581

Photography: Åsa Dahlgren
Styling: Gudrun Bonér
Makeup: Regina Törnvall
Interior design: Petra Waldersten
Original editor: Annika Ström

Translation by Carol Huebscher Rhoades

Printed in China

10 9 8 7 6 5 4 3 2 1

Table of Contents

Your best friend in the wardrobe!

I love cardigans! I think they are the world's best garment.

There is a cardigan for everyone and a cardigan for every occasion. A cardigan is a garment that brings out the best in the person wearing one. It is personable and generous. The cardigan is friendly and forgiving. Wearing a pretty cardigan is like being embraced by someone you like.

I have specifically designed the 24 cardigans in this book for people who need a cozy, functional, and nice cardigan that also expresses their work or passion.

The beauty of knitting and crocheting is that there is no rush, no time limit. You can relax as you watch your work take shape—or let your mind wander.

Another important advantage is that you can make the changes you want. Maybe you want to make the cardigan shorter or longer, add a pocket or change the collar? Don't hesitate—just do it!

I want to inspire you to create your favorite cardigan. You can choose one of the designs in the book or use parts of several patterns to create your own personal cardigan. Choose a color you like and create your own best friend for the wardrobe!

Birgitta

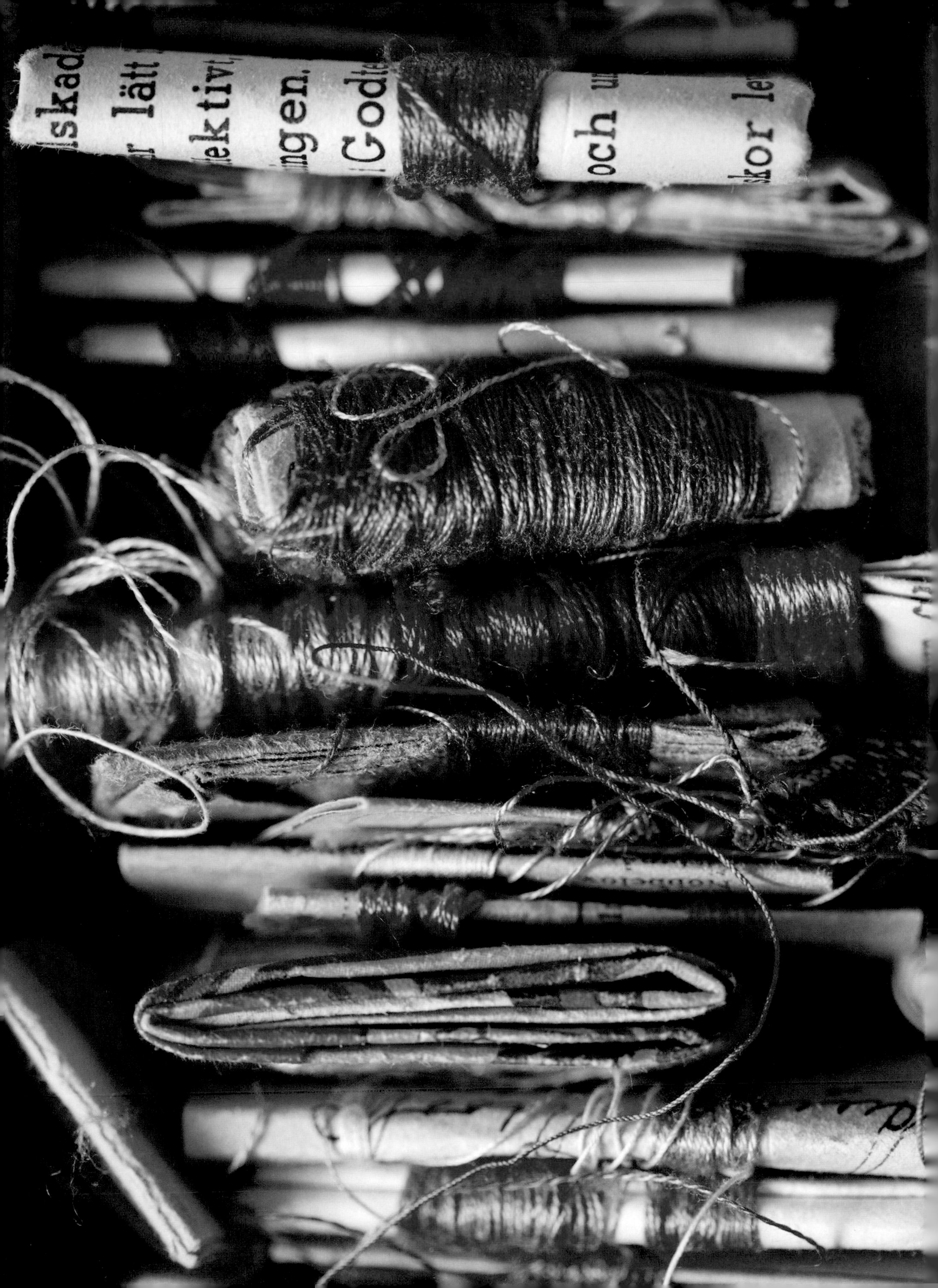

lätt
ektivt,
ngen.
och

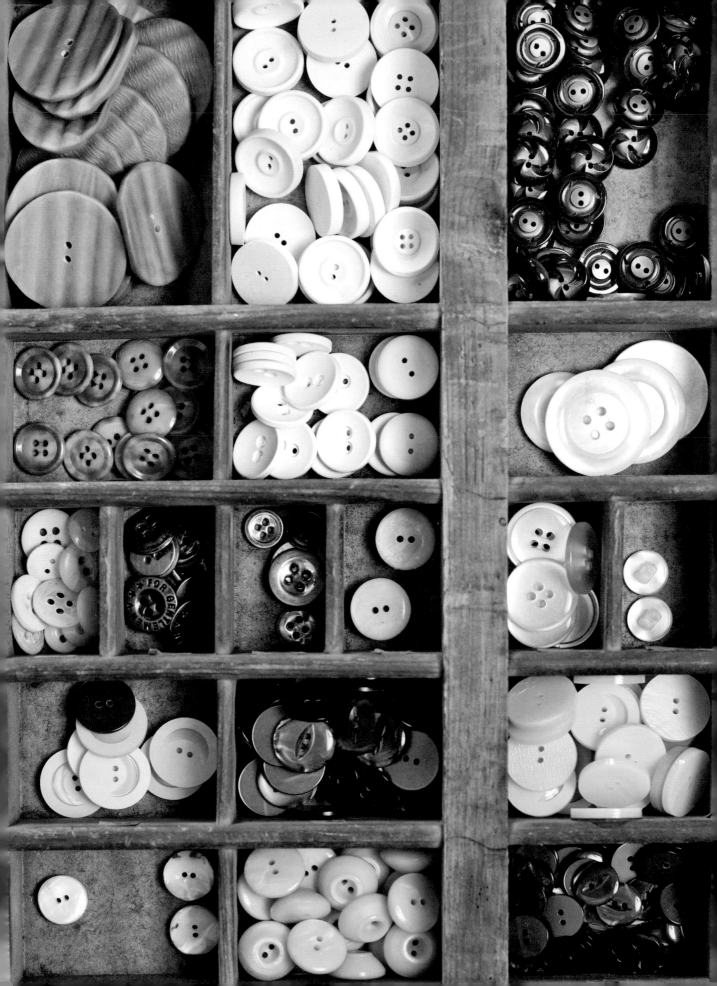

The equestrian's cardigan

A Chanel-inspired cardigan with a very effective garter stitch hound's tooth pattern. The sweater is knitted with one color at a time to avoid tangling on the wrong side. This is a sturdy cardigan that almost feels like a jacket and works just as well in the stable as on the job.

Nora practices natural horsemanship, which means that she communicates with her horses through leadership and sensitivity, not punishment.

SIZES: S (M, L)

FINISHED MEASUREMENTS
Length: 19 (19¾, 20½) in / 48 (50, 52) cm
Chest: 37¾ (40¼, 42½) in /
96 (102, 108) cm
Sleeve length: 16¼ (16½, 16¾) in /
41 (42, 43) cm

MATERIALS
Yarn: CYCA #3 (DK/light worsted),
Garnstudio Drops Karisma Superwash
(109 yd/100 m / 50 g; 100% wool)
Yarn Amounts:
Color 1: Black #05, 8 (9, 9) balls
Color 2: Off White #01, 6 (7, 7) balls
Needles: U.S. size 6 / 4 mm
Notions: 6 buttons; stitch holder
Gauge: 19 sts and 36 rows in pattern =
4 x 4 in / 10 x 10 cm.
Adjust needle size to obtain correct gauge
if necessary.

PATTERNS
SEED STITCH
Row 1: *K1, p1*; rep * to * across.
Row 2: Work purl over knit and knit over
purl.
Repeat Row 2.

HOUND'S TOOTH (multiple of 4 + 3 sts)
Note: All the stitches slipped from the
previous row are slipped on the RS.
Row 1 (Color 1, RS): Knit.
Row 2 (Color 1, WS): Knit.
Row 3 (Color 2): *K3, slip next st (Color
1) wyb*; rep * to * across and end with k3.
Row 4 (Color 2): *K3, slip next st (Color
1) wyf (the same st as slipped on previous
row)*; rep * to * across and end with k3.
Row 5 (Color 1): Knit.
Row 6 (Color 1): Knit.
Row 7 (Color 2): K1, *slip next st (Color 1)
wyb, k3*; rep * to *across and end with slip
next st wyb, k1.
Row 8 (Color 2): K1,*slip next st (Color 1)

wyf, k3*; rep * to * across and end with slip next st wyf, k1.
Repeat Rows 1-8.

INSTRUCTIONS
BACK

With Color 1, CO 83 (87, 91) sts and work back and forth in seed st for ¾ in / 2 cm. Now work in Hound's Tooth pattern, except for the 4 sts at each side which continue in seed st with Color 1 (for side slits). When piece is 1½ in / 4 cm long, increase 1 st at each side. These 2 new stitches are edge sts and knit on all following rows and are not part of the pattern; work remaining sts in Hound's Tooth pattern. When piece measures approx. 11¾ (12¼, 12¾) in / 30 (31, 32) cm, begin raglan shaping for the armhole on pattern Row 1: Work edge st, k2tog, work in pattern until 3 sts rem and end with ssk, edge st. Decrease the same way on every other row another 31 (33, 35) times. BO rem 21 sts.

LEFT FRONT

With Color 1, CO 53 (57, 61) sts and work back and forth in seed st for ¾ in / 2 cm. Now work in Hound's Tooth pattern, except for the 4 sts at the beginning of the row which continue in seed st with Color 1 (side slit) and 6 sts at the end of the row which also continue up to the neckline in seed st with Color 1 for the front band. When piece is 1½ in / 4 cm long, increase 1 st at the side for an edge st to be knit on all following rows (the edge st is not part

of the pattern); continue the 6 sts of front band in seed st with Color 1 and rem sts in Hound's Tooth pattern. When front is 4¾ in / 12 cm long, make a pocket: on RS, work 12 sts in pattern, BO the next 21 sts, place rem sts of front on a holder. Now work the pocket lining separately: CO 21 sts with Color 1 and work in stockinette for 4 in / 10 cm. Return front sts to needle and work the 21 pocket lining sts over the gap. Continue in pattern until piece measures approx. 11¾ (12¼, 12¾) in / 30 (31, 32) cm. Shape raglan armhole at the side as for back. *At the same time,* on the 24th (26th, 28th) raglan decrease, BO 13 (14, 15) sts at front edge for the neck. Next, on every other row, BO 2,2,1,1 (2,2,2,1; 3,2,2,1) sts at neck edge. When 3 sts rem, BO across.

Mark spacing for 6 buttons down front band. Place the lowest button approx. 2 in / 5 cm from bottom edge and the top button 4 rows below neckline, with the rest spaced evenly between.

RIGHT FRONT

Work as for left front, reversing shaping. Work the buttonholes on the front band, spaced as for buttons. Work each buttonhole on front band as follows: Work 2 sts, BO 2 sts, work 2 sts. On the next row, CO 2 sts over the gap.

SLEEVES

With Color 1, CO 43 (47, 47) sts and work in seed st for ¾ in / 2 cm. Now work in

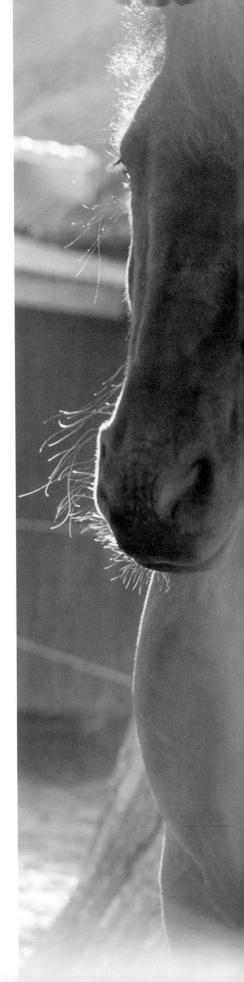

Hound's Tooth pattern, except for the 2 outermost sts at each side which continue in seed st with Color 1 for the slit. When piece is 1¼ in / 3 cm long, increase 1 st at each side for an edge st that is knitted on all following rows and is not included in the pattern. Work across in Hound's Tooth pattern for another ¾ in / 2 cm and then begin shaping sleeve: Increase 1 st inside the edge st at each side. Work new sts into pattern. Increase the same way on every 6th row until there are a total of 73 (77, 81) sts. When the sleeve measures 16¼ (16½, 17) in / 41 (42, 43) cm, shape the raglan as for the back with a total of 31 (33, 35) decrease rows. BO rem 11 sts. Make the second sleeve the same way.

FINISHING

Read the information about blocking and finishing on page 141 and then block and seam the cardigan pieces. Sew the pocket linings down neatly on WS of each front. Sew on buttons.

NECKBAND

Beginning inside one front edge, with Color 1, pick up and knit approx. 57 (61, 65) sts around the neck edge to inside of the other front edge. Work in seed st for 1¼ in / 3 cm and then BO.

POCKET BANDS

With Color 1, pick up and knit 21 sts along the bound-off sts for pocket. Work in seed st for ¾ in / 2 cm and then BO.

The barista's cardigan

This feather-light cardigan made with the softest angora yarn knits up quickly on big needles. A warm and pretty little short-sleeved cardigan that is like a piece of jewelry—perfect for everyday use and even for parties.

Evelina is a barista and coffee artist with the right touch in her fingertips. She makes sure that every brewing results in the perfect cup of coffee. In order to be called a barista, you need training, experience, and a strong passion for coffee.

SIZES: S (M, L)

FINISHED MEASUREMENTS
Length: 17¼ (18¼, 19) in / 44 (46, 48) cm
Chest: 35½ (39½, 43¼) in / 90 (100, 110) cm
Sleeve length: 2½ (2¾, 3¼) in / 6 (7, 8) cm

MATERIALS
Yarn: CYCA #3 (DK/light worsted), L.U.P. Angora (approx. 43 yd/40 m / 10 g; 80% angora, 20% wool)
Yarn Amounts: Green, 9 (10, 11) balls
Substitution: CYCA #3 (DK/light worsted) Angorella Angora (approx. 118 yd/108 m / 25 g; 80% angora, 20% merino); 4 (4, 5) balls
Needles: U.S. sizes 6 and 10 / 4 and 6 mm
Notions: 5 buttons; stitch holder
Gauge: 16 sts and 22 rows in stockinette on larger needles = 4 x 4 in / 10 x 10 cm. Adjust needle sizes to obtain correct gauge if necessary.

BACK
With smaller needles, CO 70 (78, 86) sts and work in k1, p1 ribbing for 1½ in / 4 cm. Change to larger needles and stockinette, always knitting the outermost st at each side as an edge st. When piece measures 10¼ (10¾, 11) in / 26 (27, 28) cm, BO 3,2,1,1,1 (3,2,2,1,1; 3,2,2,2,1) st at each side on every other row for the armhole = 54 (60, 66) sts rem. When armhole measures 7 (7½, 8) in / 18 (19, 20) cm, BO 7,6 (8,7; 9,8) sts on every other row at each side to shape shoulders. BO remaining sts.

LEFT FRONT
With smaller needles, CO 42 (46, 50) sts and work in k1, p1 ribbing for 1½ in / 4 cm. Change to larger needles and stockinette, always knitting the outermost st at the side as an edge st. Place the outermost 7 sts at the front edge on a holder for the front band. When at the same length, shape armhole as for back = 27 (30, 33) sts

rem. When armhole measures 3¼ (3½, 4) in / 8 (9, 10) cm, shape neck by binding off 6,4,2,1,1 (6,4,2,2,1; 6,4,3,2,1) sts on every other row. When at same length, shape shoulder as for back.

RIGHT FRONT
Work as for left front, reversing shaping.

SLEEVES
With smaller needles, CO 54 (58, 62) sts and work in k1, p1 ribbing for ¾ in / 2 cm. Change to larger needles and stockinette, always knitting the outermost st at each side as an edge st. When sleeve measures 2½ (2¾, 3¼) in / 6 (7, 8) cm, BO 3,2 sts

on every other row at each side to shape sleeve cap. Now decrease 1 st at each side on every other row 11 (12, 13) times. Next, BO 2 sts at each side on every other row 3 times. BO remaining 10 (12, 14) sts. Make the other sleeve the same way.

FINISHING
Read the information about blocking and finishing on page 141 and then block and seam cardigan.

FRONT BANDS
With smaller needles, pick up the 7 sts held for left front band. Work in k1, p1 ribbing until, when stretched slightly, the band reaches neckline. BO across. Mark the spacing for 5 buttons along front band: place lowest button 1½ in / 4 cm above lower edge and top button ⅜ in / 1 cm below neckline, with the rest spaced evenly between. Work the right front band the same way, but make buttonholes spaced as for buttons. Work each buttonhole on RS as follows: Work 2 sts, BO 2 sts, work 3 sts. On the next row, CO 2 sts over the gap. When at same length as left band, BO all sts.

NECKBAND
With smaller needles, pick up and knit 91 (97, 103) sts around the neck and work in k1, p1 ribbing for ¾ in / 2 cm. BO all sts. Sew on buttons.

The farmer's cardigan

This cardigan is easy to knit and features fine cable patterning to shape the shoulders for a good fit overall. At the same time it is practical—accommodating and roomy, just right for the farmer's constant movement on the job.

Malin is a hobby farmer. She likes the changes of season and loves following the developments of the crops, plants, and sweet little lambs. Her tractor, which has aged with its beauty intact, is a real old faithful and a huge help for all the chores that go with farming.

SIZES: S (M, L)

FINISHED MEASUREMENTS
Length: 21¾ (22½, 23¼) in /
55 (57, 59) cm
Chest: 39½ (42½, 45¾) in /
100 (108, 116) cm
Sleeve length: 17¾ (18½, 19¼) in /
45 (47, 49) cm

MATERIALS
Yarn: CYCA #3 (DK/light worsted),
Rowan Wool Cotton 4 ply (123 yd/112 m
/ 50 g; 50% Merino wool, 50% cotton)
Yarn Amounts: Sea #492, 7 (8, 8) balls
Needles: U.S. size 4 / 3.5 mm
Notions: 5 buttons
Gauge: 23 sts and 32 rows in stockinette =
4 x 4 in / 10 x 10 cm.
Adjust needle size to obtain correct gauge
if necessary.

CABLE RIB PATTERN (multiple of 5 +
2 sts)
Row 1: *P2, sl 1, k2, pass slipped st over
the 2 knitted sts*; rep * to * across, ending
row with p2.
Row 2: K2, *p1, yo, p1, k2*; rep * to *
across.
Row 3: *P2, k3*; rep * to * across, ending
row with p2.
Row 4: K2, *p3, k2*; rep * to * across.
Repeat Rows 1-4.

INSTRUCTIONS
BACK
CO 114 (121, 128) sts and work across in
stockinette, always knitting the outermost
st at each side as an edge st. Work as set for
¾ in / 2 cm. Knit 1 row on WS for foldline. Continue in stockinette for 6 rows
and then work in stripe pattern, beginning on RS: Purl 1 row, knit 2 rows, purl
2 rows, knit 2 rows, purl 1 row. Continue

in stockinette until piece measures 14¼ (14½, 15) in / 36 (37, 38) cm from foldline. Shape armhole: BO 4,2,2,1,1 (4,2,2,2,1; 4,2,2,2,2) sts on every other row at each side = 94 (99, 104) sts rem.

After completing armhole shaping, work stripe pattern, beginning on RS: Purl 1 row, knit 2 rows, purl 2 rows, knit 2 rows, purl 1 row. Work the rest of the back in Cable Rib except for the edge st at each side. When armhole measures 7½ (8, 8¼) in / 19 (20, 21) cm, shape shoulders: BO 7,7,7,7 (8,7,7,7; 8,8,7,7) sts at each side on every other row . BO remaining 38 (41, 44) sts.

LEFT FRONT

CO 65 (71, 77) sts and work across in stockinette, always knitting the outermost st at left side as an edge st. When piece measures ¾ in / 2 cm, CO 6 sts at right side for the vertical facing = 71 (77, 83) sts. Knit 1 row on WS for foldline as for back. On the next and all following RS rows, knit across to last 7 sts, sl 1 purlwise wyb (vertical foldline) and knit rem 6 sts. On all following WS rows, always purl the 7 sts, including the fold stitch. Work in stockinette until there are a total of 6 rows from foldline and then work stripe pattern as for back, continuing vertical foldline and facing as set.

When at same length as back, shape arm-hole as for back = 61 (66, 71) sts rem, and then work stripe sequence except over the 7 foldline and facing sts. Work the Cable Rib across except for the edge st at left side and the last 13 sts at right side. When the armhole measures 4¾ (5¼, 5½) in / 12 (13, 14) cm, BO 23 (25, 27) sts for neck. At neck edge, on every other row, BO 2,2,2,2,1,1 (2,2,2,2,2,2; 3,3,2,2,2,2) sts = 28 (29, 30) sts rem. When at same length, shape shoulder as for back.

Mark spacing for buttons on front edge: place lowest button 2½ in / 6 cm above horizontal foldline and align top button with the last stripe before the cable rib, with the rest spaced evenly between.

RIGHT FRONT

Work as for left front, reversing shaping and working buttonholes spaced as for buttons.

Note: The buttonholes are worked on the facing and on front edge. Beginning at the facing, work 2 sts, BO 3 sts, work 1 st, slip foldline st, work 1 st, BO 3 sts, finish row. On the next row, CO 3 sts above each gap.

SLEEVES

CO 56 (60, 64) sts and work the edge sts, stockinette, foldline, and stripe pattern as for back. When piece measures 2 in / 5 cm above foldline, increase 1 st inside the edge st at each side. Repeat this increase row every ¾ in / 2 cm another 17 (18, 19) times = 92 (98, 104) sts. When sleeve is 17¾ (18½, 19¼) in / 45 (47, 49) cm long from the foldline, BO 4 (4, 4) sts at each side for sleeve cap. Next, decrease 1 st on every other row at each side 18 (19, 20)

times and then BO 2 sts at the beginning and end of every row 7 (8, 9) times. *At the same time*, beginning on the 6th row of sleeve cap, work stripe and then cable rib pattern as for back and front. BO rem 20 (20, 20) sts after completing sleeve cap shaping. Make the other sleeve the same way.

FINISHING

Read the information about blocking and finishing on page 141 and then block and seam cardigan. On lower edge and sleeves of cardigan, fold in facings at foldlines and sew down on WS. Fold the facings on front edges at foldline and sew facings down on WS. If desired, sew neatly around buttonholes, working through both layers. Sew on buttons.

NECKBAND

Pick up and knit approx. 100 (110, 120) sts around neck, beginning and ending at fold stitches of front facings. Work 2 rows in stockinette and then work stripe pattern beginning on RS: Purl 1 row, knit 2 rows, purl 2 rows, knit 2 rows, purl 1 row and then work 10 rows stockinette. BO all sts. Fold neckband to WS and sew down.

The florist's cardigan

A quick and easily knitted cardigan. The entire sweater is worked in a type of ribbing that provides elasticity and good shaping. The knitted-in pockets are fun and a practical detail to give the cardigan character.

Jette works as a florist. She runs a flower shop and has been deepening her great love of the plant kingdom for more than fifteen years. Because her work environment can be cool and damp, she needs a cardigan that provides warmth and comfort, but at the same time looks professional when she talks to customers in the shop.

SIZES: S (M, L)

FINISHED MEASUREMENTS
Length: 20½ (21¾, 22¾) in /
52 (55, 58) cm
Chest: 39½ (41¼, 43¼) in /
100 (105, 110) cm
Sleeve length: 17 (17¼, 17¾) in /
43 (44, 45) cm

MATERIALS
Yarn: CYCA #4 (afghan/aran/worsted),
Garnstudio Drops Lima (98 yd/90 m / 50
g; 65% wool, 35% alpaca)
Yarn Amounts: Green #0705, 13 (14, 14)
balls
Needles: U.S. size 6 / 4 mm
Crochet Hook: U.S. size G-6 / 4 mm
Notions: 7 buttons; stitch holder
Gauge: 19 sts and 26 rows in pattern = 4 x
4 in / 10 x 10 cm.

Adjust needle size to obtain correct gauge if necessary.

STAGGERED RIB PATTERN (multiple of 4 sts)
Rows 1, 3, and 5: *K2, p2*; rep * to * across.
Row 2 and all even-numbered rows: Work purl over purl and knit over knit.
Rows 7, 9, and 11: *P2, k2*; rep * to * across.
Repeat Rows 1-12.

INSTRUCTIONS
BACK
CO 94 (98, 102) sts and work in pattern over all the sts, always knitting the outermost st at each side as an edge st (edge sts are not included in the pattern). After working 1 in / 2.5 cm, and then with 1 in / 2.5 in between, decrease 1 st inside edge st

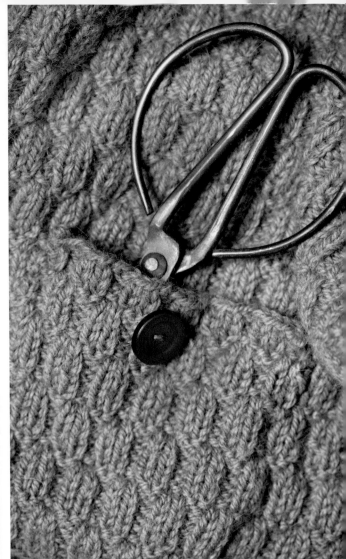

at each side a total of 4 times. When piece is 6 in / 15 cm long, increase 1 st inside the edge st at each side every 1 in / 2.5 cm a total of 4 times. Work new sts into pattern. When piece measures 13 (13¾, 14½) in / 33 (35, 37) cm, BO 6,2,2,1,1,1 (7,2,2,1,1,1); 8,2,2,1,1,1) sts on every other row at each side to shape armhole = 68 (70, 72) sts rem. When armhole measures 7 (7½, 8) in / 18 (19, 20) cm, BO 8,7,7 (8,7,7; 8,7,7) sts at each side on every other row to shape shoulders. BO rem 24 (26, 28) sts.

LEFT FRONT

CO 55 (57, 59) sts and work in pattern over all the sts, always knitting the outermost st at left side as an edge st (the edge st is not included in the pattern). Decrease and increase at the left side as for back.

At the same time, when front measures 4¾ in / 12 cm, make a pocket: Work 18 (20, 20) sts from front edge, BO the next 24 sts; put rem sts on a holder and set piece aside. Now work the pocket lining: CO 24 sts and work in stockinette for

4 in / 10 cm. Place front sts back on needle and work the pocket lining sts over the gap. Continue in pattern.

When at same length, shape armhole at left side as for back = 42 (43, 44) sts rem. When armhole measures 6 (6¼, 6¾) in/ 15 (16, 17) cm, BO 15 (16, 17) sts for neck. Next, at neck edge, BO 2,1,1,1 (2,1,1,1; 2,1,1,1) sts on every other row = 22 (22, 22) sts rem. When at same length, shape shoulder as for back. Mark spacing for 5 buttons at front edge: Place lowest button approx. 5¼ in / 13 cm above lower edge and top button approx. 1¼ in / 3 cm below neckline, with the rest spaced evenly between.

RIGHT FRONT

Work as for left front, reversing shaping. Space buttonholes as for buttons. Work buttonholes on RS rows as follows: Work 2 sts, BO 2 sts, complete row. On the next row, CO 2 sts above gap.

SLEEVES

CO 50 (54, 54) sts and work in pattern across, always knitting the outermost st at each side as an edge st (edge sts are not included in the pattern). When sleeve is 2 in / 5 cm long, increase 1 st inside edge st at each side. Increase the same way every ¾ in / 2 cm 11 (11, 13) more times = 74 (78, 82) sts. Work new sts into pattern. When sleeve is 17 (17¼, 17¾) in / 43, 44, 45) cm long, shape sleeve cap: BO 6 (7, 8) sts at each side = 62 (64, 66) sts rem.

Now decrease 1 st inside edge st on every other row at each side 14 (15, 16) times. Next, BO 3 sts at beginning of every row 4 times. BO rem 22 (22, 22) sts. Make another sleeve the same way.

FINISHING

Read the information about blocking and finishing on page 141 and then block and seam cardigan. Sew down pocket linings on WS of each front. Sew on the 5 buttons along front edge.

POCKET BANDS

Pick up and knit along the 24 bound-off sts of pocket. Make a buttonhole by working 11 sts in pattern, BO 2 sts, work 11 sts in pattern. On the next row, CO 2 new sts over the gap. Continue in pattern until band is 1¼ in / 3 cm long and then BO all sts. Sew on the button for each pocket.

CROCHETED EDGINGS

With crochet hook, work a round of single crochet all around the edges of the cardigan. Beginning on lower edge at right side seam, work along the right lower edge, continue up the right front edge and then around the neck, down left front edge, and, finally, along lower edge of cardigan to right side seam. Finish with 1 sl st into first sc.

The ballerina's cardigan

The close-fitting ballerina's cardigan overlaps to allow full movement. The seed stitch rhomboids are certainly a little time-consuming but impart a refined, classic look to the sweater. Of course, you can simplify it by working the cardigan in garter stitch or all moss stitch instead.

Saga has been dancing ballet since she was little and now her training requires daily practice. Dancing takes strength and flexibility, and it is important to keep warm with a cardigan between passes.

SIZES: S (M, L)

FINISHED MEASUREMENTS
Length: 14¼ (15, 15¾) in /
36 (38, 40) cm
Chest: 35½ (38½, 41¾) in /
90 (98, 106) cm
Sleeve length: 17¼ (17¾, 18¼) in /
44 (45, 46) cm

MATERIALS
Yarn: CYCA #1 (sock/fingering/baby),
Rowan Wool Cotton 4-ply (123 yd/112 m
/ 50 g; 50% Merino wool, 50% cotton)
Yarn Amounts: Petal #494, 6 (6, 7) balls
Needles: U.S. size 4 / 3.5 mm
Notions: Lace ribbon, approx. 45¼
(47¼, 49¼) in / 115 (120, 125) cm long;
2 lengths of grosgrain ribbon or another
similar inelastic band, 15¾ in / 40 cm and
31½ in / 80 cm
Gauge: 21 sts and 33 rows in pattern =
4 x 4 in / 10 x 10 cm.

Adjust needle size to obtain correct gauge
if necessary.

RHOMBOID PATTERN (multiple of 10 + 3
sts)
Row 1 (RS): P1, k1, p1, *k3, p1, k3, p1, k1,
p1*; rep * to * across.
Row 2: P1, k1, *p3, k1, p1, k1, p3, k1*; rep
* to * across, ending row with p1.
Row 3: K3, *k1, p1, k1, p1, k1, p1, k4*; rep
* to * across.
Row 4: P3, *k1, p1, k1, p1, k1, p1, k1, p3*;
rep * to * across.
Row 5: Work as for Row 3.
Row 6: Work as for Row 2.
Row 7: Work as for Row 1.
Row 8: P1, k1, p1,*k1, p5, k1, p1, k1, p1*;
rep * to * across.
Row 9: P1, k1, *p1, k1, p1, k3, p1, k1 p1,
k1*; rep * to * across and end row with p1.
Row 10: Work as for Row 8.
Repeat Rows 1-10.

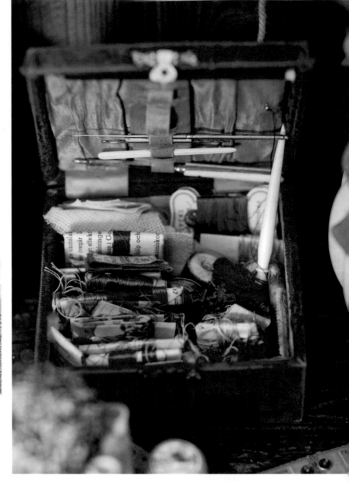

INSTRUCTIONS
BACK
CO 95 (105, 115) sts and knit 4 rows in garter st. Now work in rhomboid pattern across, always knitting the outermost st at each side as an edge st. When piece measures 7 (7½, 8) in / 18 (19, 20) cm, BO 4,2,2,1,1,1 (5,2,2,1,1,1; 6,2,2,1,1,1) sts on every other row at each side to shape armholes = 73 (81, 89) sts rem. When armhole measures 7½ (8, 8¼) in / 19 (20, 21) cm, BO 7,6,6 (8,7,6; 8,8,7) sts on every other row at each side to shape shoulders. BO rem 35 (39, 43) sts.

LEFT FRONT
CO 75 (85, 95) sts and knit 4 rows in garter st. Now work in rhomboid pattern across, always knitting the outermost st at each side as an edge st. When piece is 2 in / 5 cm long, begin shaping neckline as follows: On all RS rows, k2tog inside edge st at front edge. Decrease the same way 44 (51, 58) more times. *At the same time,* when at same length, shape armhole at left side as for back. When at same length, shape shoulder as for back.

RIGHT FRONT
Work as for left front, reversing shaping.

SLEEVES
CO 50 sts and knit in garter st for 1½ in / 4 cm. Now work in rhomboid pattern across, always knitting the outermost st at each side as an edge st.

Note: The pattern begins with 4½ moss stitch rhomboids. When sleeve measures 2 in / 5 cm, increase 1 st inside edge st at each side. Repeat this increase row every ¾ in / 2 cm 13 (16, 19) more times = 78 (84, 90) sts. Work new sts into pattern. When sleeve is 17¼ (17¾, 18¼) in / 44 (45, 46) cm long, BO 4,2,2 (5,2,2; 6,2,2) sts at each side on every other row to shape sleeve cap. Now decrease 1 st inside edge st on every other row at each side 13 (15, 17) times. Next, BO 2 sts on every other row at each side 3 times and then BO 3 sts at each side on every other row 2 times. BO rem 12 (12, 12) sts. Make second sleeve the same way.

FINISHING
Read the information about blocking and finishing on page 141 and then block and seam cardigan, except for right side. When seaming right side, leave a 1¼ in / 3 cm-long opening ⅜ in / 1 cm up from the lower edge (where the tie will be drawn through—see photo at upper left on page 38). On the wrong side, sew the lace ribbon along front edges and around back neck. Sew on the ties securely: the long band is sewn on the WS along the lower edge of left front and the short band at the corresponding place on the right front.

The minister's cardigan

It is easiest to knit a yoke-pattern sweater such as this in the round, cutting the center front open afterwards. Circular knitting makes it easy to work multi-color patterns because you can always see the pattern as it develops on the right side. Before you cut the cardigan open, machine-stitch lines to each side of the cutting line to reinforce the stitches.

Johanna is a minister who meets daily with people in both sorrow and happiness. The wonderfully soft cardigan she is wearing is sophisticated and provides a warm frame for the priest's collar on her professional working dress.

SIZES: S (M, L)

FINISHED MEASUREMENTS
Length: 20½ (21¼, 22) in / 52 (54, 56) cm
Chest: 37¾ (41, 44) in / 96 (104, 112) cm
Sleeve length: 17¾ (18¼, 18½) in / 45 (46, 47) cm

MATERIALS
Yarn: CYCA #1 (sock/fingering/baby), Rowan Cashsoft 4-ply (175 yd/160 m / 50 g; 57% Merino wool, 33% acrylic, 10% cashmere)
Yarn Amounts:
Color 1: Thunder #518, 6 (7, 7) balls
Color 2: Vamp #532, 1 ball
Color 3: Sky Pink #540, 1 ball
Color 4: Sunny #577, 1 ball
Color 5: Cream #500, 1 ball
Substitution: CYCA #1 (sock/fingering/baby), Rowan Pure Wool 4-ply (174 yd/160 m / 50 g; 100% Super Wash wool)

Needles: U.S. sizes 2-3 and 4 / 3 and 3.5 mm: Circulars 32 in / 80 cm for body and 16 in / 40 cm for sleeves. If necessary, set of 5 dpn U.S. size 2-3 / 3 mm for sleeve cuffs.
Notions: 6 buttons
Gauge: 24 sts and 32 rows in stockinette on larger needles = 4 x 4 in / 10 x 10 cm. Adjust needle sizes to obtain correct gauge if necessary.

BODY
With Color 1 and smaller size circular, CO 231 (251, 271) sts; do not join. Work back and forth in k1, p1 ribbing for 1¼ in / 3 cm. Change to larger size circular and stockinette. On the first row of stockinette, CO 6 sts at the end of the row for a steek (stitches to be cut open when finishing). Join, place marker for beginning of rnd, and continue in stockinette.
When piece measures 13 (13½, 13¾) in /

33 (34, 35) cm, shape armholes as follows: K53 (58, 63), BO 10 sts, k105, 115, 125), BO 10 sts, k53 (58, 63) and k6 for steek. Set piece aside and work sleeves.

SLEEVES

With Color 1 and short smaller size circular or dpn, CO 54 (56, 58) sts; join, being careful not to twist cast-on sts. Place marker for beg of round. Work around in k1, p1 ribbing for 1¼ in / 3 cm. Change to larger size circular and stockinette. On the first rnd, increase 10 sts evenly spaced around. When sleeve is 2¾ in / 7 cm long, increase 1 st at each side of marked st. Increase the same way every ¾ in / 2 cm another 16 (17, 18) times = 98 (102, 106) sts. When sleeve is 17¾ (18¼, 18½) in / 45 (46, 47) cm long, BO 10 sts centered at underarm for armhole = 88 (92, 96) sts rem. Make the second sleeve the same way.

YOKE

Join the sleeves and body by working the sts of one front, a sleeve, the back, second sleeve, and opposite front = 387 (415, 443) sts (not including steek). Also work the 6 steek sts but do not include them in the stitch count, patterning, or decreases for yoke. After working around for ⅜ (¾, 1¼) in / 1 (2, 3) cm, decrease 26 (30, 34) sts evenly spaced around (remember, do not work decreases into steek) = 361 (385, 409) sts rem. Work for another ⅜ in / 1 cm and then begin charted yoke pattern (see page 44).

Note: Work another pattern stitch at the end of every rnd (before the steek) so that the motif will mirror image at center front. In other words, the last st of the round will be the same as the first st of the round. Shape the yoke by decreasing as indicated on the chart. Always decrease on a single color round.

Note: Because of the decreases, the pattern motifs will not align vertically as shown on the chart.

After completing charted rows, BO the 6 steek sts. Leave rem sts on needle for the neckband which will be worked later.

CUTTING THE STEEK

Machine-stitch 2 lines close together on each side of the center of the steek. Carefully cut cardigan open between the 2 sets of machine stitching.

NECKBAND

With smaller size circular and Color 1, pick up and knit approx. 100 (105, 110) sts around neck. Work back and forth in k1, p1 ribbing for 7 rows. Purl 1 row on RS (foldline) and then work another 7 rows of k1, p1 ribbing. BO.

LEFT FRONT BAND

With smaller size circular and Color 1, pick up and knit 3 sts for every 4 rows along front edge and side of neckband. Work back and forth in k1, p1 ribbing for 7 rows. Purl 1 row on RS (foldline) and then work another 7 rows k1, p1 ribbing. BO.

Mark spacing for 6 buttons along front band. Place the lowest one approx. 1½ in / 4 cm from lower edge and the top one at neckline; space the rest evenly between.

RIGHT FRONT BAND
Work as for left front band but make buttonholes spaced as for buttons. Make buttonholes on rows 4 and 11 as follows: For each buttonhole, BO 2 sts and, on the next row, CO 2 sts over gap. This makes

buttonholes on both the band and facing because the band will be doubled at the foldline and the facing sewn down on WS. The lowest buttonhole should start 1¼ in / 3 cm from bottom edge of cardigan. Space the remaining buttonholes evenly between the first one at bottom and the top one at neckline.

Seam the underarms. Fold facings in and sew down on WS, covering cut edges. Sew on buttons.

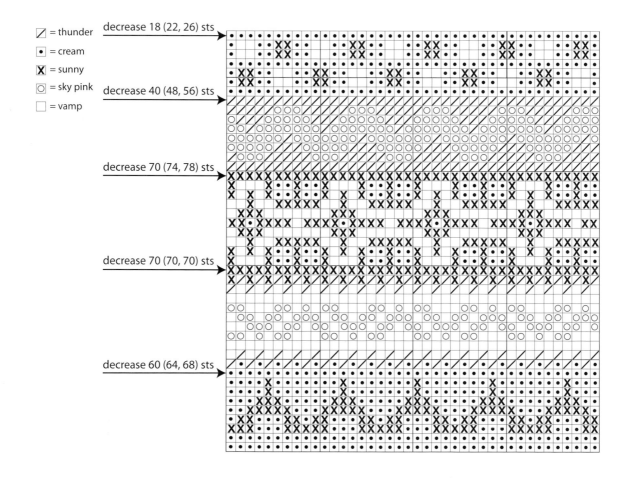

/ = thunder
• = cream
X = sunny
○ = sky pink
□ = vamp

decrease 18 (22, 26) sts

decrease 40 (48, 56) sts

decrease 70 (74, 78) sts

decrease 70 (70, 70) sts

decrease 60 (64, 68) sts

The soccer cardigan

Here's a nice stretchy cardigan worked completely in ribbing. The pattern is easy and quick to knit. Of course, you'll want to choose your favorite team's colors.

Soccer has meant a great deal for Cornelia—both on the home pitch and at competitions abroad. Traveling with the team has strengthened everyone's sense of community and friendship. Cornelia has so many wonderful memories she can look back on throughout her life. If she takes care of this cardigan, it should last just as long.

SIZES: S (M, L)

FINISHED MEASUREMENTS
Length: 19¼ (20, 21) in / 49 (51, 53) cm
Chest: 35½ (37½, 39½) in /
90 (95, 100) cm
Sleeve length: 19¾ (20½, 21¼) in /
50 (52, 54) cm

MATERIALS
Yarn: CYCA #3 (DK/light worsted),
Rowan Baby Merino Silk DK (approx. 147
yd/134 m / 50 g; 66% Merino wool, 34%
silk)
Yarn Amounts:
Color 1: Grass #685, 7 (8, 9) balls
Color 2: Snowdrop #670, 1 ball
Color 3: Sunshine #688, 1 ball
Needles: U.S. size 6 / 4 mm
Notions: separating zipper 16-18 in /
40-45 cm long
Gauge: 22 sts and 28 rows in ribbing =
4 x 4 in / 10 x 10 cm.

Adjust needle size to obtain correct gauge if necessary.

INSTRUCTIONS
BACK
With Color 1, CO 100 (106, 112) sts.
Work in k1, p1 ribbing, always knitting the outermost st at each side as an edge st. After completing 4 rows, begin color stripes. When changing colors, on the first row of each new color (always on RS), knit all the sts across. Work 8 rows Color 2, 4 rows Color 1, 8 rows Color 3.

Now continue with Color 1 only until piece measures 19 (19¾, 20½) in / 48 (50, 52) cm. BO the center 16 (18, 20) sts for back neck and work each side separately. BO another 4 sts at neck edge on every other row 2 times. BO rem 34 (36, 38) sts. Work the other side the same way, reversing shaping.

LEFT FRONT

With Color 1, CO 52 (55, 58) sts. Work in k1, p1 ribbing except for the outermost st at the side and the 2 outermost sts at center front which are edge sts and always knitted. Work the color stripes as for back and then continue with Color 1 only. When piece measures 15¾ (16¼, 16½) in / 40 (41, 42) cm, BO 6 sts at neck edge and then decrease 1 st on every other row at neck edge 12 (13, 14) times. BO rem 34 (36, 38) sts.

RIGHT FRONT

Work as for left front, reversing shaping.

SLEEVES

With Color 1, CO 58 (60, 62) sts. Work in k1, p1 ribbing, always knitting the outermost st at each side as an edge st. Work the color stripes as for back and front. When sleeve is 4 in / 10 cm long, increase 1 st inside edge st at each side. Increase the same way on every 4th row 14 more times = 88 (90, 92) sts. Now increase 1 st at each side on every other row 8 (9, 10) times and then 1 st at each side on *every* row 8 (9, 10) times = 120 (126, 132) sts. When sleeve is 19¾ (20½, 21¼) in / 50 (52, 54) cm long, BO all sts. Make the second sleeve the same way.

FINISHING

Read the information about blocking and finishing on page 141 and then block and seam cardigan.

COLLAR

With Color 1, CO 112 (116, 120) sts and work in k1, p1 ribbing in the following color sequence: 2 rows Color 1, 2 rows Color 3, 2 rows Color 1, 2 rows Color 2, 2 rows Color 1, 2 rows Color 3, and 2 rows Color 1. **Note:** On RS rows, when changing to a new color, knit across.
At the same time, on Row 9 (after a stripe with Color 2), BO 8 (9, 10) sts at each side. Repeat this decrease on the next row. After the last stripe with Color 1, BO all sts. Make another collar piece the same way but with Color 1 only. With RS facing RS, sew the two collar pieces together along the two short sides and outer edge. Turn RS out and sew collar as invisibly as possible around neck.

Sew in zipper.

The potter's cardigan

This cardigan with a simple lace pattern offers plenty of freedom of movement for creativity and combines well with jeans or a nice dress. The tweed yarn we've used here gives structure to the sweater; but if you choose a cotton yarn instead the lace pattern will show a little more clearly.

Hannah throws both clay and stoneware and fires her pots traditionally or as raku. All of her work is unique and her creativity is driven by the desire to express beauty, humor, and simplicity in her pieces.

SIZES: S (M, L)

FINISHED MEASUREMENTS
Length: 22 (22¾, 23¾) in / 56 (58, 60) cm
Chest: 37½ (39½, 41¼) in / 95 (100, 105) cm
Sleeve length: 15¾ (16¼, 16½) in / 40 (41, 42) cm

MATERIALS
Yarn: CYCA #4 (afghan/aran/worsted), Rowan Felted Tweed Aran (191 yd/175 m / 50 g; 50% Merino wool, 25% alpaca, 25% viscose)
Yarn Amounts: Dark Violet 738, 8 (9, 10) balls
Crochet Hook: U.S. size G-6 / 4 mm
Notions: 8 buttons
Gauge: 4 pattern groups and 10 pattern group rows = 4 x 4 in / 10 x 10 cm.
Adjust needle size to obtain correct gauge if necessary.

PATTERN (multiple of 5 + 4 sts)
Row 1: Skip 3 ch, *work (3 dc, ch 1, 1 dc) in next st = 1 st-group, skip 4 ch*; rep * to * across, ending with 1 dc in last ch. Turn with ch 3.
Row 2: *Work (3 dc, ch 1, 1 dc = 1 st-group) around ch of previous row's st-group*; rep * to * across, ending with 1 dc at top of t-ch.
Repeat Rows 1-2.

INSTRUCTIONS
BACK
Ch 99 (104, 109) and work in pattern, beginning with Row 1 = 19 (20, 21) st-groups. When piece measures 14½ (15, 15½) in / 37 (38, 39) cm, shape armholes. First, decrease for the armholes by working slip sts over 1 st-group at the beginning of the row and, at the end of the row, do not work last st-group. Now decrease 1 st at each side on every row 4 times (after

these decreases, another st-group has been eliminated) = 15 (16, 17) st-groups rem. When armhole measures 7½ (8, 8¼) in / 19 (20, 21) cm, skip the 5 (6, 7) st-groups at the center for the back neck and work each shoulder separately. Shape the shoulder and neck on the next row by working slip sts over the outermost st-group and leaving the last st-group at the end of the row unworked. On the last row, work 1½ st-groups and end the row at the center of the shoulder with 1 sl st. Cut yarn. Work the other shoulder the same way, reversing shaping.

LEFT FRONT
Ch 51 (54, 56) and work in pattern = 9 (10, 10) st-groups.

Note: On sizes S and L, end the first row at the front edge with 3 dc instead of 1 dc. Begin the next row with 2 dc (the ch 3 turning ch = 1 dc).
When at same length, shape armhole as for back. When armhole measures 5½ (6, 6¼) in / 14 (15, 16) cm, sl st over 2 (3, 3) st-groups for neck. On sizes S and L, decrease the 3 dc at the front edge. Next, decrease 1 dc on every row 4 times at neck edge (= eliminating 1 more st-group). When at same length, shape shoulder as for back.

RIGHT FRONT
Work as for left front, reversing shaping.

SLEEVES
Ch 44 (49, 54) and work in pattern = 8 (9,

10) st-groups. After ⅜ in / 1 cm, inc 1 dc at each side. Increase the same way on every other row until there are 14 (15, 16) st-groups; work new sts into pattern. When sleeve is 15¾ (16¼, 16½) in / 40 (41, 42) cm long, shape sleeve cap by working slip sts over 1 st-group at the beginning of the row and leaving last st-group of row unworked. Next, decrease 1 dc at each side on every row 9 (10, 11) times and then decrease 2 dc at each side on every row 6 (7, 8) times. Cut yarn. Make another sleeve the same way.

FINISHING

Read the information about blocking and finishing on page 141 and then block and seam cardigan.

POCKETS (make 2 alike)

Ch 39 and work in pattern (7 st-groups) for 5¼ in / 13 cm. Cut yarn.

POCKET FLAPS

Ch 39 and work in pattern (7 st-groups). On the 3rd row, make a buttonhole as follows: Work 3 st-groups, ch 3, skip 1 st-group, work 3 st-groups. On the next row, work 1 st-group around the ch loop. Work 1 more row (= 5 rows total). Cut yarn.

COLLAR

Ch 104 (114, 119) and work in pattern = 21 (22, 23) st-groups for 2¼ in / 5.5 cm. Cut yarn.

CROCHETED EDGING

Work 5 rows of single crochet all around the cardigan except for the neck.

Row 1: Beginning at top left neck, sc down left front edge, work 3 sc at corner, sc along lower edge, 3 sc at corner, and sc up right front edge, ending at neck. Cut yarn.

Row 2: Work as for Row 1 but through back loops only. Work 3 sc into the center st at each corner. Cut yarn.

Row 3: Work as for Row 2, but make 6 buttonholes along right front band: For each buttonhole, ch 2 and skip 2 sc. Place the bottom buttonhole 2 ¾ in / 7 cm from lower edge and the top one ¾ in / 2 cm from neck edge, with the rest spaced evenly between.

Row 4: Work as for Row 2 and, for each buttonhole, work 2 sc around ch loop. Cut yarn.

Row 5: Work as for Row 2. Cut yarn.

Work 5 rnds of sc through back loops around edge of each sleeve. Finish with 2 rows sc around the collar and each pocket flap.

Sew on collar. Sew on pockets and pocket flaps. Sew on buttons.

Midsummer cardigan

An old-fashioned camisole inspired our midsummer cardigan. This one is knitted with a lovely light cotton yarn and can be worn without an undershirt or blouse underneath if you like. The ribbed pattern and the five gores at the lower edge help the cardigan fit the figure well.

Isabella has celebrated a traditional midsummer in the Swedish archipelago since she was a child. During the summers she goes there as often as possible to enjoy the salt air and the light-filled evenings.

SIZES: S (M, L)

FINISHED MEASUREMENTS

Length: 20 (21, 21¾) in / 51 (53, 55) cm
Chest: 32¼ (34¾, 37) in / 82 (88, 94) cm
Sleeve length: 12¾ (13, 13½) in / 32 (33, 34) cm

MATERIALS

Yarn: CYCA #3 (DK/light worsted), Garnstudio Drops Muskat (109 yd/100 m / 50 g; 100% cotton)
Yarn Amounts: White #18, 9 (10, 10) balls
Needles: U.S. size 6 / 4 mm
Crochet Hook: U.S. size G-6 / 4 mm
Notions: 6 buttons
Gauge: 21 sts and 28 rows in pattern = 4 x 4 in / 10 x 10 cm.
Adjust needle size to obtain correct gauge if necessary.

SEED STITCH

Row 1: *K1, p1*; rep * to * across.
Row 2: Work purl over knit and knit over purl.

Repeat Rows 1-2.

PATTERN (multiple of 3 + 1 sts)

Row 1 (RS): *K1, p2*; rep * to *, ending row with k1.
Row 2 and all even-numbered rows: Knit.
Repeat Rows 1-2.

INSTRUCTIONS
BACK

CO 150 (156, 162) sts and work 6 rows in seed st. Change to pattern except over the gores, which are worked in stockinette as follows: K1 (edge st which is knitted on every row and not included in pattern), 16 sts pattern, 24 sts stockinette, 22 (25, 28) sts pattern, 24 sts stockinette, 22 (25, 28)

sts pattern, 24 sts stockinette, 16 sts pattern, k1 (edge st, always knitted and not included in pattern). Shape the gores by working k2tog at the beginning and end of each gore on every other row until 2 sts remain for each gore. Now work all gore sts into pattern = 84 (90, 96) sts rem. When piece measures 12¾ (13, 13½) in / 32 (33, 34) cm, shape armhole: BO 3,2,2,2 (4,2,2,2; 5,2,2,2) sts on every other row at each side = 66 (70, 74) sts rem. When armhole measures 7 (7½, 8) in / 18 (19, 20) cm, BO the center 20 (22, 24) sts for neck. Work each side separately.

At neck edge, BO 2 sts on every other row 3 times and, *at the same time*, when armhole measures 7½ (8, 8¼) in / 19 (20, 21) cm, BO 6,6,5 (6,6,6; 7,6,6) sts on every other row for shoulder. Work the other shoulder the same way, reversing shaping.

LEFT FRONT

CO 70 (73, 76) sts and work 6 rows in seed st. Change to pattern except for the gores worked in stockinette as follows: K1 (edge st which is knitted on every row and not included in pattern), 19 (22, 25) sts pattern, 24 sts stockinette, 19 sts pattern, 7 seed sts (for front band). Shape the gore as for the back = 48 (51, 54) sts rem. After completing gores, continue in pattern between the edge st at side and the 7 seed sts of front band.

When at same length, shape armhole as for back = 39 (41, 43) sts rem. When arm-hole measures 4 (4¼, 4¾) in / 10 (11, 12) cm, BO 13 (14, 15) sts for neck and then decrease 1 st at neck edge on every other row 9 times. When at same length, shape shoulder as for back.

Mark spacing for 6 buttons along front band: Place bottom button 2¾ in / 7 cm from lower edge and top button about ¾ in / 2 cm below neckline, with the rest spaced evenly between.

RIGHT FRONT

Work as for left front, reversing shaping. Make buttonholes spaced as for buttons. Make buttonholes as follows: On RS, work 2 sts, BO 3 sts, complete row. On the next row, CO 3 sts over the gap.

SLEEVES

CO 45 (48, 51) sts and work in seed st for 6 rows. Now work in pattern, always knitting the outermost st at each side as an edge st; edge sts are not included in the pattern. When sleeve is 2¾ in / 7 cm long, increase 1 st inside edge st at each side. Increase the same way every ¾ in / 2 cm, 7 (8, 9) more times = 61 (66, 71) sts. Work new sts into pattern. When sleeve is 12¾ (13, 13½) in / 32 (33, 34) cm long, begin shaping sleeve cap. BO 3 (4, 5) sts at each side. Next, decrease 1 st at each side on every other row 13 (14, 15) times and then BO 2 sts at beginning of next 8 rows. BO rem 13 (14, 15) sts. Make the other sleeve the same way.

FINISHING

Read the information about blocking and finishing on page 141 and then block and seam cardigan. Sew on buttons.

CROCHETED EDGINGS

Work 1 row of sc along the outer edges of the cardigan.

The beach cardigan

This cardigan features a brilliant and fun pattern. It is easy to knit because you only work with one color at a time and only in garter stitch. Slip stitches produce this very effective pattern.

Emelie absolutely loves the 1950s aesthetic. Here she is enjoying the sun, the life on the rocky beach, and swimming, but when the sun goes behind the clouds, she likes cuddling up in her cotton cardigan because it is so practical. The sweater can also be worn as a short bathrobe.

SIZES: S (M, L)

FINISHED MEASUREMENTS
Length: 22½ (23¼, 24) in / 57 (59, 61) cm
Chest: 39½ (41¼, 43¼) in /
100 (105, 110) cm
Sleeve length: 19¼ (19¾, 20) in /
49 (50, 51) cm

MATERIALS
Yarn: CYCA #3 (DK/light worsted),
Rowan Handknit Cotton (93 yd/85 m /
50 g; 100% cotton)
Yarn Amounts:
Color 1: Turkish Plum #277, 9 (9, 10) balls
Color 2: Bleached #263, 6 (6, 7) balls
Needles: U.S. sizes 4 and 7 / 3.5 and
4.5 mm
Gauge: 19 sts and 30 rows in pattern on
larger needles = 4 x 4 in / 10 x 10 cm.
Adjust needle sizes to obtain correct gauge
if necessary.

PATTERN (multiple of 4 + 3 sts)
Row 1, Color 2 (RS): K1, *sl 1 wyb, k3*;
rep * to * and end with sl 1, k1.
Row 2, Color 2: K1, *sl 1 wyf, k3*; rep * to
* and end with sl 1, k1.
Row 3, Color 1: *K3, sl 1 wyb*; rep * to *
and end with k3.
Row 4, Color 1: *K3, sl 1 wyf*; rep * to *
and end with k3.
Repeat Rows 1-4.

INSTRUCTIONS
BACK
With larger needles and Color 1, CO 97
(101, 105) sts. Purl 1 row (= WS) and then
work in pattern, always knitting the outermost st at each side as an edge st. After
2 in / 5 cm, increase 1 st inside edge st at
each side. Increase the same way every 2
in / 5 cm 3 more times = 105 (109, 113) sts.
Work new sts into pattern. When piece
measures 21¾ (22½, 23¼) in / 55 (57, 59)
cm, shape shoulders: BO 5,5,6,6,6,6,6

(5,6,6,6,6,6,6; 6,6,6,6,6,7,7) sts on every other row at each side. BO remaining sts.

LEFT FRONT

With larger needles and Color 1, CO 36 (36, 40) sts and purl 1 row (= WS). Work in pattern, always knitting the outermost st at left side as an edge st. Increase at the left side as for back = 40 (40, 44) sts. When at same length, shape shoulder as for back.

RIGHT FRONT

Work as for left front, reversing shaping.

SLEEVES

With larger needles and Color 1, CO 45 (45, 49) sts and purl 1 row (= WS). Now work in pattern except the outermost st at each side which is always knitted as an edge st. After working for 2¾ in / 7 cm, increase 1 st inside edge st at each side.

Increase the same way every ¾ in / 2 cm 19 (20, 21) more times = 85 (89, 93) sts. When sleeve is 19¼ (19¾, 20) in / 49 (50, 51) cm long, BO all sts. Make the second sleeve the same way.

FINISHING

Read the information about blocking and finishing on page 141 and then block and seam cardigan.

FRONT BANDS

With RS facing, smaller needles and Color 1, pick up and knit approx. 110 (120, 130) sts along right front and to center of back neck. Work in k1, p1 ribbing for 3¼ (3½, 3½) in / 8 (9, 9) cm. BO all sts. Work the left side the same way, beginning at center back neck. Seam short ends of band at center back neck.

The tango bolero

This stockinette stitch bolero has a long cable edging that is worked separately and then sewn on. The cable strip adds weight to the edges and helps the bolero hold its shape. The garment came into its own in the nineteenth century when the bolero dance was introduced, but at that time the jacket was worn only by cavaliers.

Valentina and Gustaf are professional competition dancers and well-established at the top of the world rankings. They have received excellent scores in both national and international competitions and are also the dance masters in their own dance studio.

SIZES: S (M, L)

FINISHED MEASUREMENTS
Length: 16¼ (17, 17¾) in / 41 (43, 45) cm
Chest: 35½ (37½, 39½) in /
90 (95, 100) cm
Sleeve length: 17¾ (18¼, 18½) in /
45 (46, 47) cm

MATERIALS
Yarn: CYCA #2 (sport/baby), Hjertegarn Alpaca Silk (180 yd/165 m / 50 g; 60% alpaca, 30% Merino wool, 10% silk)
Yarn Amounts: Black 500, 6 (6, 7) balls
Needles: U.S. size 2-3 / 3 mm and cable needle
Gauge: 26 sts and 34 rows in stockinette = 4 x 4 in / 10 x 10 cm.
Adjust needle size to obtain correct gauge if necessary.

INSTRUCTIONS
BACK
CO 102 (110, 118) sts and work in stockinette, always knitting the outermost st at each side as an edge st. When piece is for 2 in / 5 cm long, increase 1 st inside edge st at each side. Increase the same way every ¾ in / 2 cm 5 more times = 114 (122, 130) sts. When piece measures 8¾ (9, 9½) in / 22 (23, 24) cm, shape armhole: BO 5,2,2,1,1 (6,2,2,2,1; 7,2,2,2,2) sts at each side on every other row = 92 (96, 100) sts rem. When armhole measures 7½ (8, 8¼) in / 19 (20, 21) cm, BO 5,5,5,5,5 (6,5,5,5,5; 6,6,5,5,5) sts at each side for the shoulders.
At the same time as the 3rd decrease for shoulders, BO the center 34 (36, 38) sts for back neck and then work each side separately. At neck edge, BO another 2,2 sts on every other row. Work the other shoulder as for the first, reversing shaping.

LEFT FRONT

CO 24 (28, 32) sts and work in stockinette, always knitting the outermost st at each side as an edge st. Increase 2 sts inside edge st (k1, p1, k1 into same st) at front edge on rows 4, 6, 8, 10, 12, and 14. Next, increase 1 st inside edge st at front edge on every other row 17 (18, 19) times. *At the same time,* increase at the left side when at same length as on back = 59 (64, 69) sts.

When at same length, shape armhole as for back. When piece measures 9 (9½, 9¾) in / 23 (24, 25) cm, decrease 1 st inside edge st at front edge on every other row 23 (25, 27) times = 25 (26, 27) sts. When at same length, shape shoulder as for back.

RIGHT FRONT

Work as for left front, reversing shaping.

SLEEVES

CO 52 (54, 56) sts and work in k1, p1 ribbing for 3¼ in / 8 cm. Change to stockinette, always knitting the outermost st at each side as an edge st. Increase 1 st inside edge st at each side every ⅜ in / 1 cm 20 (22, 24) times = 92 (98, 104) sts. When sleeve is 17¾ (18¼, 18½) in / 45 (46, 47) cm long, shape sleeve cap. First BO 5 (6, 7) sts at each side and then decrease 1 st inside edge st at each side on every other row 18 (19, 20) times. Next, BO 2 sts at each side on every other row 6 times. BO

rem 22 (24, 26) sts. Make the second sleeve the same way.

FINISHING

Read the information about blocking and finishing on page 141 and then block and seam cardigan.

CABLE BAND

CO 20 sts.

Rows 1, 3, and 5 (RS): K1, p1, k8, p1, sl 1 wyb (foldline), k8.

Rows 2, 4, 6, and 8: Work knit over knit and purl over purl except for the outermost st at each side which is knitted as an edge st. Purl the foldline st that was slipped on RS.

Row 7: K1, p1, place the next 4 sts on cable needle and hold in front of work, k4 and then k4 from cable needle, p1, sl 1 wyb, k8.

Repeat Rows 1-8.

Make the cable band long enough to fit around the sweater from the center back, down right front edge, along lower edge, up left front, back to center back—approx. 80⅔ (84⅔, 88½) in / 205 (215, 225) cm long.

With RS facing, seam the cable band to the bolero's edges beginning at center back. After sewing on band, fold along slip st foldline and sew the edge down on WS.

The longboard cardigan

Here's a different sort of sweater for anyone who likes to knit and crochet! The front pieces are crocheted from side to side while the back, sleeves, and pocket linings are knitted. The crochet front makes the sweater sturdier than other sweaters, so it is more like a jacket.

Joel loves to skate on his longboard and it goes with him whenever he travels out of the country. For him, longboarding is the perfect way to become familiar with a new city because he can get around quickly and know the city like a native in almost no time.

SIZES: S (M, L)

FINISHED MEASUREMENTS
Length: 26 (26¾, 27½) in /
66 (68, 70) cm
Chest: 39½ (41½, 45¾) in /
100 (108, 116) cm
Sleeve length: 19 (19¼, 19¾) in /
48 (49, 50) cm

MATERIALS
Yarn: CYCA #3 (DK/light worsted),
Rowan Tweed (129 yd/118 m / 50 g; 100%
wool)
Yarn Amounts:
Color 1: Askrigg #585, 7 (8, 9) balls
Color 2: Muker #587, 3 (3, 3) balls
Needles: U.S. size 6 / 4 mm
Crochet Hook: U.S. size G-6 / 4 mm
Notions: 5 buttons
Gauge: 17 sc and 19 rows = 4 x 4 in /
10 x 10 cm

20 sts and 30 rows in stockinette = 4 x 4 in
/ 10 x 10 cm.
Adjust needle/hook size to obtain correct
gauge if necessary.

INSTRUCTIONS
RIGHT FRONT
Color sequence:
Begin with 3 rows with Color 1.
Work 2 rows with Color 2 and then alternate colors with 2 rows each throughout.

The front begins at the side. With Color 1,
ch 71 (73, 75). Beginning in 2nd ch from
hook, work 1 sc in each ch = 70 (72, 74) sc.
Turn each row with ch 1. Crochet the rest
of the front with 1 sc in each sc, working
in the color sequence above.
Begin shaping armhole on the 4th row by
working 1 sc, 2 sc in the next sc, and then
1 sc in each sc to end of row. On the next
row, sc across until 2 sts rem, work 2 sc

in next st and then 1 sc in last st. Increase the same way with 1 new st on every row 3 more times.

At the end of the 9th row, ch 32 (34, 36) to complete armhole. Turn and begin with 1 sc in the 2nd ch from hook. Continue in sc across = 106 (110, 114) sc.

On the 11th (13th, 15th) row, begin a pocket opening: Work 15 sts from lower edge; turn and work back. Continue working back and forth over 15 sts for a total of 26 rows. Cut yarn.

Now work on the front back and forth, starting at the 16th st from lower edge and up towards the shoulder for a total of 26 rows. After completing pocket opening, work across all sts from lower edge to shoulder.

At the same time, shape shoulder on the 15th (17th, 19th) row: Work until 2 sts rem, work 2 sc in same st and end with 1 sc. Increase for the shoulder the same way on Rows 19, 23, 27, 31, 35 (21, 25, 29, 33, 37; 23, 27, 31, 35, 39). On Row 38 (40, 42), begin shaping V-neck, decreasing on every other row: Sc from lower edge until 15 sts rem; turn and sc back. Work until 3 sts rem; turn and work back. Continue with 3 fewer sts on alternate rows another 4 (5, 6) times. Cut yarn.

LEFT FRONT
Work as for right front, reversing shaping.

BACK
The back is knitted from the lower edge up. With Color 1, CO 105 (110, 115) sts. Work in stockinette, always knitting the outermost st at each side as an edge st. After working in stockinette for 1¼ in / 3 cm, knit 1 row on WS for foldline. Continue in stockinette until, as measured from foldline, back is 1¼ in / 3 cm longer than front pieces to beginning of armhole. BO 4,2,2 sts at each side on every other row for armholes = 89 (94, 99) sts rem. When armhole is the same length as for fronts, shape shoulders, beginning at sides: BO 5,5,4,4,4,4,4 (5,5,5,5,4,4,4; 5,5,5,5,5,5,4) on every other row at each side. BO remaining sts.

SLEEVES
With Color 1, CO 57 (59, 61) sts. Work in stockinette, always knitting the outermost st at each side as an edge st. After working in stockinette for 1¼ in / 3 cm, knit 1 row on WS for foldline. Continue in stockinette for ¾ in / 2 cm after foldline and then begin sleeve shaping: Increase 1 st inside edge st at each side every ¾ in / 2 cm 20 (21, 22) times = 97 (101, 105) sts. When sleeve is 19 (19¼, 19¾) in / 48 (49, 50) cm from foldline, shape sleeve cap: decrease 1 st on every other row at each side 5 times and then BO 5 sts at each side on every other row 7 times. BO remaining sts. Make the second sleeve the same way.

FINISHING AND POCKET LININGS
Read the information about blocking and finishing on page 141 and then block and

seam cardigan. Fold facings in and sew down on WS. The front pieces will be approx. 1¼ in / 3 cm shorter than the back. **For pocket linings:** With Color 1, CO 28 sts and work in stockinette for 3½ in / 9 cm. BO all sts. Make another pocket lining the same way. Sew pocket linings into place on WS, from top edge of opening.

CROCHETED EDGINGS

With Color 1, beginning at lower edge of right front, sc up front edge, around neck, down left front, and then around lower edge. Work 3 sc in each corner, at lower edges of fronts and at base of V-neck, on every row. Mark spacing for 5 buttons along right front band: Place lowest button about 4 in / 10 cm from lower edge and top button about ¾ in / 2 cm below base of V-neck, with the rest spaced evenly between. On the 3rd row, make buttonholes along left front band spaced as for buttons: For each buttonhole, ch 3 and skip 3 sc. On the next row, work 3 sc around ch loop. Work a total of 5 rows on edging; cut yarn. Sew side seams at lower edge. Finally, with Color 1, work 26 sc across top of each pocket. Work a total of 3 rows and cut yarn.

The violinist's cardigan

This beautiful lace-patterned cardigan has a special construction—it is worked in two identical pieces. You begin at the cuff and increase to the front and back sections. Both pieces are sewn together with a seam down the center back and then the sides and sleeves are seamed.

Sara is the first concert master and violinist in a large symphony orchestra. Her shoulders must be covered during concert performances. The cardigan's wide sleeves allow for full movement while the sweater keeps her shoulders beautifully warm at the same time.

SIZES: S-M (M-L)

FINISHED MEASUREMENTS
Length: 12¼ (13¾) in / 31 (35) cm
Chest: 35½ (39½) in /
90 (100) cm
Sleeve length: 21 (22) in / 53 (56) cm

MATERIALS
Yarn: CYCA #3 (DK/light worsted), Garnstudio Drops Cotton Viscose (120 yd/110 m / 50 g; 54% cotton, 46% rayon viscose)
Yarn Amounts: Dark Green #12, 8 (9) balls
Needles: U.S. sizes 2-3 and 4 / 3 and 3.5 mm
Crochet Hook: U.S. size D-3 / 3 mm
Notions: 1 button; stitch holder
Gauge: 23 sts and 30 rows in pattern on larger needles = 4 x 4 in / 10 x 10 cm.

Adjust needle sizes to obtain correct gauge if necessary.

PATTERN (multiple of 5 sts)
Row 1: K1, *k2tog, yo, k3*; rep * to * and end row with k2tog, yo, k2.
Row 2 and all following WS rows: Purl.
Row 3: *K2tog, yo, k1, yo, ssk*; rep * to * across.
Row 5: K5, *yo, k2tog, k3*; rep * to * across.
Row 7: K3, *k2tog, yo, k1, yo, ssk*; rep * to * across and end with k2.
Repeat Rows 1-8.

INSTRUCTIONS
LEFT SLEEVE, FRONT AND BACK
With smaller needles, CO 58 (64) sts. Work back and forth in k1, p1 ribbing for 6 in / 15 cm. Change to larger needles and purl 1 row on WS, increasing 54 (58) sts

evenly spaced across between edge sts = 112 (122) sts. Begin working in pattern, always knitting the outermost st at each side as an edge st (edge sts are not included in pattern). When piece measures 26½ (28) in / 67 (71) cm, divide piece into 2 equal sections that are worked separately. Work the back first, placing sts for front on a holder.

At neck edge, decrease 1 st on every 4th row 4 times. When piece measures 4 (5¼) in / 10 (13) cm after the split for back/front, BO rem 52 (57) sts of back. Place sts for front on needle. At neck edge, BO 6 sts and then, on every other row, BO 2 sts at neck edge 9 (11) times. When piece measures 4 (5¼) in / 10 (13) cm, BO rem 32 (33) sts.

RIGHT SLEEVE, FRONT AND BACK

Work as for left sleeve, front and back, reversing shaping.

FINISHING

Read the information about blocking and finishing on page 141 and then block and seam cardigan at center back. Seam sleeves from the ribbed edge and up for 21 (22) in / 53 (56) cm.

RIBBED LOWER EDGE

With smaller needles, pick up and knit 184 (196) sts along lower edge and work back and forth in k4, p2 ribbing (RS rows end with k4) for 2¾ (3½) in / 7 (9) cm. BO all sts.

CROCHETED EDGINGS

Beginning at lower right front, work in sc up right front, around neck, and down left front edge. Now work 3 rows as follows: on all rows, at corner where center front slants diagonally for neck, work 3 sc in corner st. On the 1st row, make 1 button-hole about ¾ in / 2 cm below neckline as follows: Ch 3 and skip 3 sc. On the next row, work 3 sc around ch loop. Work the 3rd and final row and then cut yarn. Sew on button to left side centered as for buttonhole.

The garden cardigan

Here's a beautiful cardigan worked only with knit stitches. The striped look is structured with slip stitches. My inspiration for this model was the classic Higgins cardigan worn by Professor Higgins in the musical My Fair Lady. *The elbow patches are just the right finishing touch, aren't they?*

Magnus and Karolina have been given the pleasure of taking over Magnus's grandmother's old small farm with a cottage. The little garden is full of berry bushes; other fruits and vegetables, such as strawberries and potatoes, are grown as well.

SIZES: S (M, L)

FINISHED MEASUREMENTS
Length: 26¾ (28¼, 30) in / 68 (72, 76) cm
Chest: 40½ (43¼, 45¾) in /
103 (110,116) cm
Sleeve length: 18¼ (19, 19¾) in /
46 (48, 50) cm

MATERIALS
Yarn: CYCA #3 (DK/light worsted),
Rowan Felted Tweed DK (191 yd/175 m /
50 g; 50% Merino wool, 25% alpaca,
25% rayon)
Yarn Amounts: Phantom 153, 10 (11, 12)
balls
Needles: U.S. size 4 / 3.5 mm
Crochet Hook: U.S. size E-4 / 3.5 mm
Notions: 5 buttons and 2 elbow patches
Gauge: 24 sts and 30 rows in pattern = 4 x
4 in / 10 x 10 cm.

Adjust needle size to obtain correct gauge if necessary.

PATTERN (multiple of 4 + 2 sts)
Row 1 (WS): *K2, sl 2 wyf*; rep * to *
across, ending with k2.
Row 2 (and all RS rows): Knit.
Repeat Rows 1-2.

INSTRUCTIONS
BACK
CO 120 (128, 136) sts and purl 1 row on RS. Now work in pattern, always knitting the outermost st at each side as an edge st. When piece measures 19 (19¾, 20½) in / 48 (50, 52) cm, shape armhole: On each side on every other row, BO 6,2,1,1,1,1 (6,2,2,2,1,1; 6,2,2,2,2,2) sts = 96 (100, 104) sts rem. When armhole measures 8¼ (8¾, 9) in / 21 (22, 23) cm, BO 5,5,5,5,5,5,2 (5,5,5,5,5,5,3; 5,5,5,5,5,5,4)

sts on every other row at each side for shoulders.

At the same time, on the 4th shoulder decrease, BO the center 20 (22, 24) sts for back neck and work each side separately. At neck edge, on every other row, BO 3,3 sts. Work the other side the same way, reversing shaping.

RIGHT FRONT

CO 64 (68, 72) sts and purl 1 row on RS. Now work in pattern, always knitting the outermost st at right side as an edge st. The outermost 8 sts at the left edge (center front) will form the button band. When at same length, shape armhole as for back = 52 (54, 56) sts rem.

At the same time, when working first decrease for the armhole, begin shaping V-neck on RS: K2tog inside the 8 sts for button band and then complete row in pattern. Decrease the same way for neck on every 8th row 11 (12, 13) more times. When at same length, shape shoulder as for back and then continue working the 8 button band sts for another 2½ (2¾, 3) in / 6.5 (7, 7.5) cm. BO.

Mark spacing for 5 buttons down front band: Place lowest button approx. 4¼ in / 11 cm above lower edge and top button ⅜ in / 1 cm below base of V-neck, with the rest spaced evenly between.

LEFT FRONT

Work as for right front, reversing shaping. Make buttonholes spaced as for buttons. Make each buttonhole as follows: Work 3 sts on RS, BO 3, complete row. On the next row, CO 3 sts over gap.

SLEEVES

CO 68 (72, 76) sts and purl 1 row on RS. Work sleeve in pattern, always knitting the outermost st at each side as an edge st. When sleeve is 4 (4¼, 4¾) in / 10 (11, 12) cm long, increase 1 st inside edge st at each side. Increase the same way every ¾ in / 2 cm 9 more times = 88 (92, 96) sts. Work new sts into pattern whenever there is an even number of sts on the needle. When sleeve measures 18¼ (19, 19¾) in / 46 (48, 50) cm, begin shaping sleeve cap: first, BO 6 sts at each side and then decrease 1 st on every other row at each side 15 (16, 17) times. Next, BO 3 sts at beginning of every row 12 times.

BO rem 10 (12, 14) sts. Make the second sleeve the same way.

POCKETS (make 2 alike)

CO 28 sts and work in pattern (inside an edge st at each side) for 4 in / 10 cm and then knit ¾ in / 2 cm in garter st. BO.

FINISHING

Read the information about blocking and finishing on page 141 and then block and seam cardigan. Sew the pockets to each front, with the lower edge aligned with lower edge of front. Seam the short ends of button/buttonhole bands at center back neck. Sew on buttons and then sew on elbow patches.

CROCHETED EDGING

Work a row of sc around the front edges and neck. Begin at lower edge of right front and then around the neck and down left front.

The flower cardigan

Here's a sweet cotton cardigan worked in double crochet. To add some distinction to the sweater, we've decorated it with crocheted bands, flowers, and leaves. The belt holds in the waist for a more tailored look.

Karolina and Magnus take care of his grandmother's little farm. There are, of course, lots of chores, but there's also time to enjoy the plucked berries and resplendent flowers. The cottage has a little room where they can take shelter against a rain shower or relax after working in the garden.

SIZES: S (M, L)

FINISHED MEASUREMENTS
Length: 20½ (21¼, 22) in / 52 (54, 56) cm
Chest: 35½ (37½, 39½) in /
90 (95, 100) cm
Sleeve length: 15¾ (16½, 17¼) in /
40 (42, 44) cm

MATERIALS
Yarn: CYCA #3 (DK/light worsted),
Garnstudio Drops Muskat (109 yd/100 m
/ 50 g; 100% cotton)
Yarn Amounts:
Color 1: Off White #08, 14 (15, 15) balls
Color 2: Apple Green #53, 1 ball
Color 3: Bordeaux #41, 1 ball
Crochet Hook: U.S. size G-6 / 4 mm
Notions: 5 buttons (approx. ¾ in / 2 cm
diameter with shanks on back)
Gauge: 18 sts and 12 rows in dc = 4 x 4 in
/ 10 x 10 cm.

Adjust needle size to obtain correct gauge
if necessary.

INSTRUCTIONS
BACK
With Color 1, ch 83 (87, 91). Beginning
in 4th ch from hook, work 1 dc in each
ch. Turn every row with ch 3. Continue
with 1 dc in each st. When piece measures 13 (13½,13¾) in / 33 (34, 35) cm,
shape armhole at each side as follows: Sl
st over the first 5 (6, 7) sts at beginning
of row and leave 5 (6, 7) sts unworked at
end of row. Decrease 1 dc the same way at
beginning and end of every row 2 times.
When armhole measures 7½ (8, 8¼) in /
19 (20, 21) cm, shape shoulders as follows:
Sl st over the first 10 sts, work 12 (13, 14)
dc and cut yarn. Skip 22 dc and work the
other shoulder the same way, reversing
shaping. Cut yarn.

LEFT FRONT

With Color 1, ch 43 (45, 47) and work as for back. When at same length, shape armhole at left side as for back. When armhole measures 6 (6¼, 6¾) in / 15 (16, 17) cm, shape neck: Sl st over first 6 dc. Next, decrease 1 dc at neck edge on every row 5 times. When at same length, shape shoulder as for back. Cut yarn.

RIGHT FRONT

Work as for left front, reversing shaping.

SLEEVES

With Color 1, ch 43 (45, 47) and work in dc as for back and front. After completing 6 rows, increase 1 dc at each side by working 2 dc each in the first and last dc of the row. Increase the same way on every other row 9 (10, 11) more times = 60 (64, 68) sts. When sleeve is 15¾ (16½, 17¼) in / 40 (42, 44) cm long, shape sleeve cap as follows: Sl st over the first 5 (6, 7) dc and, at the end of the row, leave 5 (6, 7) sts unworked. Decrease 1 dc at each side on every row 11 (12, 13) times. Now decrease as follows on every 4th row: 1 sl st over 1st dc, 1 dc in next dc, skip 1 dc, dc to last 3 sts, skip 1 dc, 1 dc in next st, leave last dc unworked. Cut yarn. Make second sleeve the same way.

FINISHING

Read the information about blocking and finishing on page 141 and then block and seam cardigan, leaving the last 2 in / 5 cm from lower edge open on each side (slits).

CROCHETED EDGINGS

With Color 1, work 3 rows dc as described below. Beginning at lower left front, work up to and around the neck and down right front (do not work across lower edge). **Note:** At each corner, work 3 dc in the same st (and on the following rows, work 3 dc in the center corner st).

On the 2nd row, make 6 buttonholes along right front band: for each buttonhole, ch 1, and skip 1 dc. On the next row, work 1 dc around ch loop. Place the lowest buttonhole 2¾ in / 7 cm from lower edge and the top one ⅜ in / 1 cm below neckline, with the rest spaced evenly between. Cut yarn after completing Row 3.

BELT

With Color 1, ch 13. Beginning in 4th ch from hook, work 1 dc in each ch. Turn each row with ch 3. Continue back and forth in dc until belt is approx. 22½ (23¾, 24¾) in / 57 (60, 63) cm long. Work 1 rnd of sc around the edges of the belt. Cut yarn.

BELT LOOPS (make 2 alike)

With Color 1, ch 13. Beginning in 2nd ch from hook, work 1 sc in each ch across to last st, end with 2 sc in last ch. Work back along the other side of the foundation chain, ending with 2 sc in 1st ch. Cut yarn.

DECORATIVE BANDS

With Color 2, chain a band about 86⅔ (90½, 94⅔) in / 220 (230, 240) cm long. Measure all the way around the cardigan to make sure the chain band will be long enough to fit. Beginning in the 2nd ch from hook, work 1 sc in each ch across to last ch and work 2 sc in last ch. Work back in sc along the other side of the foundation chain; cut yarn. Sew the band around the cardigan about ⅝ in / 1.5 cm in from the outer edges, beginning and ending at center back neck.

Crochet 2 more bands, each approx. 11 in / 28 cm long and sew to sleeve cuffs about ⅝ in / 1.5 cm above lower edge.

DECORATIVE LEAVES

With Color 2, ch 10 and work as follows: 1 sl st each into 2nd and 3rd ch, 1 sc in 4th ch, 1 dc each in 5th and 6th ch, 1 sc in 7th ch, and 1 sl st each into 8th and 9th ch. Ch 1 and work the same way along other side of foundation chain. Cut yarn and make another 9 leaves the same way.

ROSE

With Color 3, ch 17.

Row 1: Work 1 dc in 5th ch from hook, *ch 1, skip 1 ch, 1 dc, ch 1, 1 dc in next ch*; rep * to * across.

Row 2: Ch 3, work 5 dc in 1st ch loop, *1 sc in next ch loop, 6 dc in next ch loop*; rep * to *, ending row with 6 dc in last ch loop. Cut yarn.

Swirl the strip into a rose shape and secure with stitching at the lower edge.

Make 4 more roses the same way.

COVERED BUTTONS

Crochet a cover and place a button with a shank inside. Make cover as follows:

Ch 3 and join into a ring with 1 sl st to 1st ch.

Rnd 1: Ch 1, work 5 sc around rind and join with 1 sl st to 1st sc.

Rnd 2: Ch 1, *2 sc through back loop only in every sc around; end with 1 sl st to 1st sc.

Rnd 3: Ch 1, *1 sc through back loop in every sc around; end with 1 sl st to 1st sc.

Rnd 4: Ch 1, *1 sc through back loop in every other sc around*; end with 1 st st to 1st sc.

Cut yarn. Place button inside the cover and stitch through cover to secure.

Make 4 more button covers the same way. Sew on buttons.

Sew the top and bottom edges of belt loops at side seams. Draw the belt through the straps and sew down each short end at the center of the respective front. Securely sew the roses and leaves where the belt is attached and at center back. Sew remaining leaves and roses on each side of the neck (see photos).

The swagger cardigan

A beautiful, three-quarter length sweater that is quite wide at the lower edge and drapes well. The extra width is achieved through knitted gussets. You might want to use markers or yarn rings to mark off the gussets for easier knitting.

Lisa is a food designer who picks her ingredients from nature and the "pantry" in the garden. From her harvest, she conjures forth wonderfully tasty apple pies or entire buffets of dainties. As you can see, Lisa is in a condition that makes this roomy cardigan particularly perfect for her!

SIZES: S (M, L)

FINISHED MEASUREMENTS
Length: 25½ (26½, 27¼) in /
65 (67, 69) cm
Chest: 35½ (37½, 39½) in /
90 (95, 100) cm
Sleeve length: 17¾ (18¼, 18½) in /
45 (46, 47) cm

MATERIALS
Yarn: CYCA #3 (DK/light worsted),
Rowan Wool Cotton (123 yd/112 m / 50
g; 50% Merino wool, 50% cotton)
Yarn Amounts:
Color 1: Marine #495, 10 (11, 11) balls
Color 2: Rich #493, 2 (2, 2) balls
Needles: U.S. size 4 / 3.5 mm
Notions: 1 button; stitch holder
Gauge: 24 sts and 32 rows in stockinette
st = 4 x 4 in / 10 x 10 cm.
Adjust needle size to obtain correct gauge
if necessary.

SEED STITCH PATTERN
Row 1: *K1, p1*; rep * to * across.
Row 2: Work purl over knit and knit over purl.
Repeat Row 2.

INSTRUCTIONS
BACK
With Color 2, CO 144 (150, 156) sts and work in seed st for 1¼ in / 3 cm. Change to Color 1 and stockinette, always knitting the outermost st at each side as an edge st. When piece measures 3¼ in / 8 cm, begin shaping the gussets: On RS, k1 (edge st), k27 (29, 31), k2tog, k18 (gusset), k2tog, k44 (46, 48), k2tog, k18 (gusset), k2tog, k27 (29, 31), k1 (edge st). Decrease at beginning and end of each gusset with k2tog on every 4th row another 9 times = 104 (110, 116) sts rem.
At the same time, when piece measures 4 in / 10 cm, decrease 1 st inside edge st at

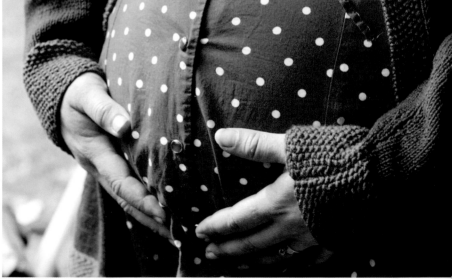

each side. Decrease the same way at each side every 1½ in / 4 cm 2 more times = 98 (104, 110) sts. When piece measures 18¼ (18½, 19) in / 46 (47, 48) cm, begin shaping armholes: BO 5,3,2,1 (6,3,2,1; 7,3,2,1) sts on every other row at each side = 76 (80, 82) sts rem. When armholes measure 7½ (8, 8¼) in / 19 (20, 21) cm, BO 7,7,7,7 (8,7,7,7; 8,8,7,7) sts at each side on every other row to shape shoulders. BO rem 20 (22, 22) sts.

LEFT FRONT

With Color 2, CO 80 (84, 88) sts and work in seed st for 1¼ in / 3 cm. Change to Color 1 and stockinette, always knitting the outermost st at left side as an edge st. Place the outermost 8 sts on right side on a holder for button band. When piece measures 3¼ in / 8 cm, begin shaping a gusset: on RS, k1 (edge st), k27 (29, 31), k2tog, k18 (gusset), k2tog, k22 (24, 26). Decrease at beginning and end of gusset with k2tog on every 4th row another 9 times = 52 (56, 60) sts rem.
At the same time, when at same length, shape side and armhole as for back = 38 (41, 44) sts rem.
When armhole measures 5¼ (5½, 5½) in / 13 (14, 14) cm, at neck edge, BO 3,2,2,2,1 (3,2,2,2,2,1; 3,2,2,2,2,1) sts on every other row. When at same length, shape shoulder as for back.

RIGHT FRONT

Work as for left front, reversing shaping.

SLEEVES

With Color 2, CO 52 (56, 60) sts and work in seed st for 2½ in / 6 cm. Change to Color 1 and stockinette st, always knitting the outermost st at each side as an edge st. Every 1¼ in / 3 cm, increase 1 st inside edge st at each side 7 (8, 9) times = 66 (72, 78) sts. When sleeve is 17¾ (18¼, 18½) in / 45 (46, 47) cm long, begin shaping sleeve cap: BO 5 (6, 7) sts at each side. Next, decrease 1 st inside edge st at each side on

every 4th row 5 (5, 5) times and then decrease 1 st at each side on every other row 4 (6, 8) times. Finally, BO 2 sts on every other row at each side 6 (6, 6) times. BO rem 14 (14, 14) sts. Make the second sleeve the same way.

FRONT BANDS

Pick up the 8 sts set aside on left front and, with Color 2, work in seed st until, when slightly stretched, the band reaches neckline. BO.
Work the right front band the same way, but, make a buttonhole approx. ¾ in / 2 cm below neckline: on RS, work 2 sts, BO 3 sts, work 3 sts. On the next row, CO 3 sts over gap. When right band is same length as left band, BO all sts.

FINISHING

Read the information about blocking and finishing on page 141 and then block and seam cardigan. Sew front bands to fronts and then sew on button.

COLLAR

With Color 2, beginning and ending inside front bands, pick up and knit approx. 62 (66, 70) sts around neck. Work in seed st for 1¼ in / 3 cm and then BO.

The artist's cardigan

The rose motif featured on this cardigan was taken from a nearly century-old cross stitch book. The motif was originally designed for a large embroidered cloth. Knitting patterns in two colors is somewhat time-consuming, but on the other hand it is fun to see how the design develops as you knit.

Regina was the make-up artist for this book. She has an amazing sensitivity to people's beauty and is always able to bring out the best in her models. When she has free time, she likes to pick up another type of brush and paint on canvas.

SIZES: S (M, L)

FINISHED MEASUREMENTS
Length: 20 (21, 21¾) in / 51 (53, 55) cm
Chest: 39 ½ (41¼, 43¼) in / 100 (105, 110) cm
Sleeve length: 17¼ (17¾, 18¼) in / 44 (45, 46) cm

MATERIALS
Yarn: CYCA #1 (sock/fingering/baby), Rowan Pure Wool 4 Ply (174 yd/159 m / 50 g; 100% superwash wool)
Yarn Amounts:
Color 1: Kiss #436, 6 (6, 7) balls
Color 2: Porcelaine #451, 4 (4, 4) balls
Needles: U.S. sizes 2-3 and 4 / 3 and 3.5 mm
Notions: 6 buttons; stitch holder
Gauge: 24 sts and 34 rows in stockinette on larger needles = 4 x 4 in / 10 x 10 cm. Adjust needle sizes to obtain correct gauge if necessary.

INSTRUCTIONS
BACK
With smaller needles and Color 1, CO 104 (112, 120) sts and work in k1, p1 ribbing for 1½ in / 4 cm. Change to larger needles and work in stockinette, always knitting the outermost st at each side as an edge st (edge sts are not included in the pattern). *At the same time*, increase 9 sts evenly spaced across 1st row = 113 (121, 129) sts. After working 4 rows in stockinette, begin working pattern on Chart A. Repeat the small cross motif until you begin working Chart B. When piece measures 3½ (4, 4¼) in / 9 (10, 11) cm, increase 1 st inside edge st at each side. Increase the same way every 1½ in / 4 cm 4 (4, 4) more times = 123 (131, 139) sts. Work new sts into pattern. When piece measures 12¼ (12¾, 13) in / 31 (32, 33) cm, shape armholes: BO 4,3,2,2,1,1 (5,3,2,2,1,1; 6,3,2,2,1,1) sts on every other row at each side = 97 (103, 109) sts rem.

When armhole measures 1½ (1¾, 2) in / 4 (4.5, 5) cm, begin rose motif following Chart B, making sure pattern is centered across back.

Note: The color symbols for Chart B are the opposite of those on Chart A. Center the motifs so that the center st of the rose pattern is also the center st on the back. After completing charted rows, continue with Color 2 only.

When armhole measures 7½ (8, 8¼) in/ 19 (20, 21) cm, shape shoulders: BO 7,7,7,6,6 (7,7,7,7,7; 8,8,7,7,7) sts at each side. BO rem 31 (33, 35) sts.

LEFT FRONT

With smaller needles and Color 1, CO 62 (66, 70) sts and work in k1, p1 ribbing for 1½ in / 4 cm. Change to larger needles and stockinette, always knitting the outermost st at left side as an edge st (the edge st is not included in the pattern). Place the outermost 10 sts at front edge on a holder. *At the same time*, increase 5 sts evenly spaced across rem sts = 57 (61, 65) sts. After working 4 rows, begin pattern on Chart A as for back. When at same length, increase at left side and shape armhole as for back. When armhole measures 1½ (1¾, 2) in /

4 (4.5, 5) cm, begin rose motif following Chart C.

Note: Center the rose motif with its center st matching center st of front.

When armhole measures 5½ (5¾, 6) in / 14 (14.5, 15) cm, BO 10 (10, 10) sts for neck. At neck edge, decrease 1 st on every row 6 (7, 8) times = 33 (35, 37) sts rem. When at same length, shape shoulder as for back.

RIGHT FRONT

Work as for left front, reversing shaping.

SLEEVES

With smaller needles and Color 1, CO 52 (54, 56) sts and work in k1, p1 ribbing for 1½ in / 4 cm. Change to larger needles and work in stockinette, always knitting the outermost st at each side as an edge st (edge sts are not included in the pattern). *At the same time,* increase 40 (44, 48) sts evenly spaced across inside edge sts = 92 (98, 104) sts. After working 4 rows, begin pattern on Chart A, continuing small cross motif throughout sleeve. When sleeve is 17¼ (17¾, 18¼) in / 44 (45, 46) cm long, shape sleeve cap: BO 4 (5, 6) sts at each side. Next, decrease 1 st inside edge st at each side on every other row 18 (20, 22) times and then BO 2 sts at beginning of every row 14 times. BO rem 20 (20, 20) sts. Make the second sleeve the same way.

FINISHING

Read the information about blocking and finishing on page 141 and then block and seam cardigan. Ease in the sleeve cap, puckering it at shoulder to fit armhole (see photos to left).

FRONT BANDS

With smaller needles and Color 1, pick up the 10 left front band sts from holder and work in k1, p1 ribbing until band, when slightly stretched, reaches neckline. BO. Mark spacing for 6 buttons down band: Place lowest button approx. 2 in / 5 cm above lower edge and top button ¾ in / 2 cm below neckline, with the rest spaced evenly between.

Work the right front band the same way but make buttonholes spaced as for buttons as follows: on RS, work 3 sts, BO 4 sts, work 3 sts. On the next row, CO 4 sts over the gap.

NECKBAND

With smaller needles and Color 1, pick up and knit approx. 84 (88, 90) sts around the entire neck, including both front bands. Work in k1, p1 ribbing for ¾ in / 2 cm. Knit 1 row on WS and then work another ¾ in / 2 cm in ribbing. BO all sts. Turn neckband at foldline and sew down on WS. Sew on buttons.

CHART A

$\boxed{\diagup}$ = porcelaine

$\square$ = kiss

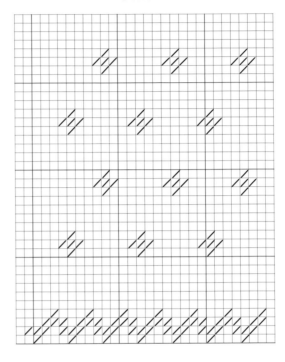

CHART C

$\square$ = porcelaine

$\boxed{\diagup}$ = kiss

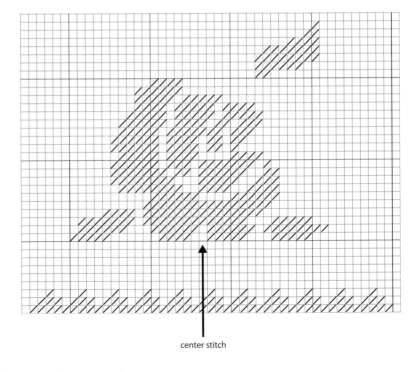

center stitch

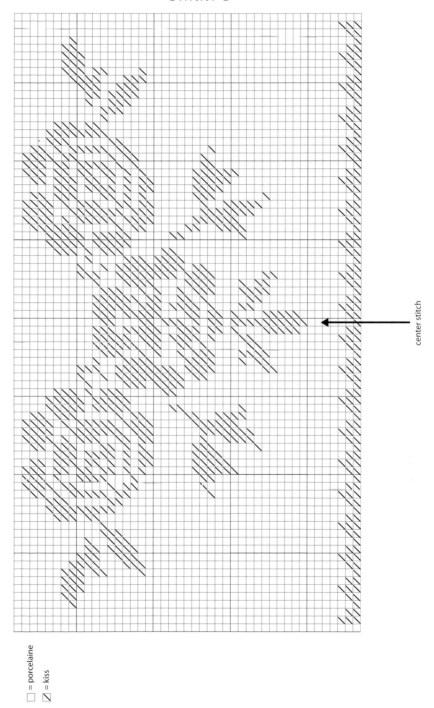

center stitch

☐ = porcelaine
◪ = kiss

The rigging cardigan

A new variation on the classic Icelandic sweater, knitted with a durable, easy-care cotton blend yarn. Of course, you can knit this cardigan with wool yarn for a warmer sweater. The sweater is easy to knit in the round; you cut the front opening afterwards and sew in the zipper.

Rigger Jens has rigged several 18th century sailing ships, but this time Jens and a team of creative adventurers have cast their lot with the Wind Wagon, a replica of an American wheel ship from the 19th century.

SIZES: S (M, L)

FINISHED MEASUREMENTS
Length: 24½ (25¼, 26) in / 62 (64, 66) cm
Chest: 37½ (39½, 41¼) in /
95 (100, 105) cm
Sleeve length: 20½ (21, 21¼) in /
52 (53, 54) cm

MATERIALS
Yarn: CYCA #4 (afghan/aran/worsted),
Rowan All Seasons Cotton (98 yd/90 m /
50 g; 60% cotton, 40% acrylic)
Yarn Amounts:
Color 1: Storm #251, 8 (9, 9) balls
Color 2: Denim #249, 1 ball
Color 3: Iceberg #192, 1 ball
Color 4: Organic #178, 1 ball
Needles: U.S. sizes 7 and 9 / 4.5 and 5.5
mm: circulars 16 in / 40 cm for sleeves and
32 in / 80 cm for body. Set of 5 dpn U.S.
size 7 / 4.5 mm for sleeve cuffs.

Notions: separating zipper, 24-25 in /
60-65 cm long
Gauge: 16 sts and 23 rows in stockinette
on larger needles = 4 x 4 in / 10 x 10 cm.
Adjust needle sizes to obtain correct gauge
if necessary.

BODY
With Color 1 and smaller size circular,
CO 145 (153, 161) sts and work back and
forth in k1, p1 ribbing for 1¼ in / 3 cm.
Change to larger size circular and stockinette. *At the same time,* CO 6 sts at the end
of the row for the steek (stitches to be cut
open when finishing). Join, being careful not to twist. Work around until piece
measures 15¾ (16½, 17¼) in / 40 (42, 44)
cm and then shape armholes: K31 (33, 35),
BO 10 sts, k63 (67, 71), BO 10 sts, k31 (33,
35) = 125 (133, 141) sts rem, and then knit
the 6 steek sts. Set piece aside while you
knit the sleeves.

SLEEVES

With Color 1 and smaller size circular or dpn, CO 36 (38, 40) sts; join, being careful not to twist cast-on row. Place marker for beginning of rnd. Work around in k1, p1 ribbing for 1¼ in / 3 cm. Change to larger size circular and stockinette, and, *at the same time,* on the first round, increase 4 sts evenly spaced around. When sleeve measures 3¼ in / 8 cm, increase 1 st on each side of the marked st. Increase the same way every 1½ in / 4 cm 5 (6, 7) more times = 52 (56, 60) sts. When sleeve is 20½ (21, 21¼) in / 52 (53, 54) cm long, BO 10 sts centered at underarm = 42 (46, 50) sts rem. Make the second sleeve the same way.

YOKE

Join the body and sleeves by knitting one front, a sleeve, the back, the second sleeve, and other front = 209 (225, 241) sts total; k6 for steek (steek sts are not included in stitch totals). Continue with Color 1 for ¾ (1¼, 1½) in / 2 (3, 4) cm and then work following the chart.

Note: Make sure that the end stitch of the rnd (not including steek) matches the beginning st so the patterning is mirror-imaged.

Decrease as indicated on the chart, always decreasing on a single-color rnd.

Note: Because of the decreases, the motifs won't necessarily align one above the other as shown on the chart.

After completing charted rows, BO steek sts. Leave rem sts on the needle for neck to be worked later.

Machine-stitch 2 lines close together on each side of the center of the steek. Carefully cut cardigan open between the 2 sets of machine stitching.

NECKBAND

With smaller size circular, work rem sts of yoke in k1, p1 ribbing for 1½ in / 4 cm. Purl 1 row on RS (foldline) and then work in k1, p1 ribbing for another 1½ in / 4 cm. BO all sts.

Read information about blocking on page 141. Seam underarms. Turn the neckband at foldline and sew down on WS along neck line. Sew in zipper.

decrease 16 (16, 16) sts

decrease 12 (14, 16) sts

decrease 12 (14, 16) sts

decrease 16 (20, 24) sts

decrease 18 (18, 18) sts

decrease 20 (23, 26) sts

decrease 22 (23, 24) sts

decrease 16 (16, 16) sts

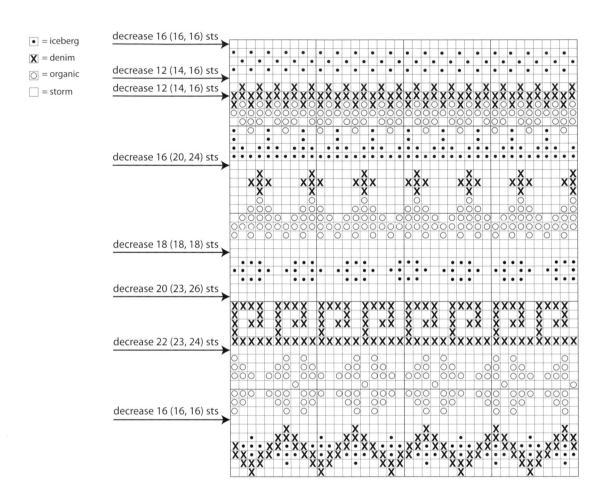

The forest cardigan

A cardigan or a coat? A little of each, actually. The top section is crocheted in a pattern that is more compact than that of the pleated lower section, which is relatively open. This long cardigan will keep your legs beautifully warm. Despite its length, the cardigan crochets up quickly.

Veronica loves nature and outdoor life. She enjoys going into the forest to pick berries and mushrooms, or just to relax.

SIZES: S (M, L)

FINISHED MEASUREMENTS
Length: 37¾ (41, 44) in /
96 (104, 112) cm
Chest: 39½ (41¼, 43¼) in /
100 (105, 110) cm
Sleeve length: 17¼ (17¾, 18¼) in /
44 (45, 46) cm

MATERIALS
Yarn: CYCA #4 (afghan/aran/worsted),
Debbie Bliss Donegal Luxury Tweed
Aran (93 yd/85 m / 50 g; 85% wool, 15%
angora)
Yarn Amounts:
Color 1: Purple #41, 12 (14, 16) skeins
Color 2: Silver #10, 6 (6, 7) skeins
Crochet Hook: U.S. size 7 / 4.5 mm
Notions: 6 clasp and hook sets
Gauge: 14 sts and 15 rows in Pattern A =
4 x 4 in / 10 x 10 cm.
Adjust hook size to obtain correct gauge if
necessary.

PATTERN A (multiple of 3 + 1 sts)
Row 1: 1 sc, *1 dc in each of next 2 sts, 1
sc in next st*; rep * to * across. Turn with
ch 2.
Row 2: *1 dc over sc, 1 sc in each of next 2
dc*; rep * to * and end row with 1 dc. Turn
with ch 1.
Repeat Rows 1-2, making sure that a dc is
worked over a sc and sc over dc.

PATTERN B (multiple of 3 + 1 sts)
Row 1: 1 dc in 3rd ch from hook, *ch 1,
skip 1 ch, 2 dc in next ch*; rep * to * across
and turn with ch 3.
Row 2: *2 dc around ch loop, ch 1*; rep * to
* across, ending with 1 dc around ch loop
of previous row. Turn with ch 3.
Repeat Row 2.

INSTRUCTIONS
BACK, TOP SECTION
With Color 1, ch 68 (74, 80). Beginning
in 2nd ch from hook, work 1 sc in each ch
= 67 (73, 79) sc. Now work Pattern A until

piece measures 8 (8¼, 8¾) in / 20 (21, 22) cm and then shape armholes: Sl st over the first 5 (5, 5) sts and leave last 5 (5, 5) sts of row unworked. On the next row, decrease 2 (2, 3) sts at beginning and end of row and then decrease 1 (2, 2) sts at each side. When armhole measures 7½ (8, 8¼) in / 19 (20, 21) cm, shape shoulders on every row with 5,5,5 (6,5,5; 6,6,5) fewer sts at each side. Cut yarn.

LEFT FRONT, TOP SECTION

With Color 1, ch 35 (38, 41). Beginning in 2nd ch from hook, work 1 sc in each ch = 34 (37, 40) sc. Now work Pattern A until same length as back to armhole. Shape armhole at side as for back. When armhole measures 6 (6¼, 6¾) in / 15 (16, 17) cm, decrease 7,2,2 (7,3,2; 7,3,3) sts on every row for neck. When at same length, shape shoulder as for back.

RIGHT FRONT, TOP SECTION

Work as for left front, reversing shaping.

SLEEVES

Note: *Increase* by working 2 sc or 2 dc (depending on pattern) in the first and last sts of the increase row. Work new sts into pattern.
Note: *Decrease* by working slip sts over sts to be eliminated at beginning of row and leaving sts unworked at end of row.
With Color 1, ch 35 (35, 38); turn and, beginning in 2nd ch from hook, work 1 sc in

each ch = 34 (34, 37) sc. Now work Pattern A until piece is 2½ in / 6 cm long. Increase (see Note above) 1 st at each side and then increase the same way on every 4th row 10 (11, 11) times = 56 (58, 61) sts.
When sleeve measures 17¼ (17¾, 18¼) in / 44 (45, 46) cm, decrease (see Note above) 5 (5, 5) sts at each side for sleeve cap = 46 (48, 51) sts.
Continue, decreasing 1 st at the beginning and end of every row 19 (20, 21) times. Cut yarn.
Make the second sleeve the same way.

PLEATED BACK

With Color 1, ch 83 (89, 95). Work 30 (32, 34) rows in Pattern B and then work stripe sequence: 7 rows Color 2, 3 rows Color 1, 3 rows Color 2, 3 rows Color 1, 7 rows Color 2 and 2 rows Color 1. Cut yarn.

PLEATED FRONTS

With Color 1, ch 39 (42, 45). Work 30 (32, 34) rows in Pattern B and then work stripe sequence: 7 rows Color 2, 3 rows Color 1, 3 rows Color 2, 3 rows Color 1, 7 rows Color 2, and 2 rows Color 1. Cut yarn.
Make the second front the same way.

FINISHING

Read the information about blocking and finishing on page 141 and then block and seam top sections of sweater. Seam the sides between the pleated back and front sections. Make sure that the extra fabric on the back is folded to form a pleat at

center back. The pleat on each front should be folded in approx. 2¾ in / 7 cm from side seam. Make sure that the side seams on top and pleated sections align exactly. Sew down the pleats along seams of top and bottom sections.

COLLAR

Work approx. 54 (58, 62) sc through both loops around the neck: Work 2 rows with Color 1, 5 rows with Color 2, 1 row with Color 1. Next, with Color 1, work 1 row of sc through back loops only (foldline). Continue in sc through both loops: 1 row with Color 1, 5 rows with Color 2, 2 rows with Color 1. Cut yarn. Turn the collar at foldline and sew down on WS.

Sew the 6 clasps and hooks evenly spaced down the front of the sweater.

SLEEVE EDGINGS

Work in sc around the lower edge of each sleeve: 2 rows with Color 1, 5 rows with Color 2, and 2 rows with Color 1. Cut yarn. Fold edgings up to RS.

The poet's cardigan

This is a comfy sweater that fits nicely at the waist and shoulders because of the smock pattern. It may take a little time to learn the smock pattern, but not very long. The rest of the sweater is worked in easy stockinette so you can relax and let your mind wander as you knit.

Olivia is a poet and performer who has won multiple poetry slams in Sweden. She tours a lot—usually alone, but sometimes with her poetry orchestra of four string musicians.

SIZES: S-M (M-L)

FINISHED MEASUREMENTS
Length: 21¼ (22 ¾) in / 54 (58) cm
Chest: 43¼ (47¼) in / 110 (120) cm
Sleeve length: 17¼ (17¾) in / 44 (45) cm

MATERIALS
Yarn: CYCA #2, Garnstudio Drops Alpaca (182 yd/166 m / 50 g; 100% alpaca)
Yarn Amounts: Light Pearl Gray #9020, 7 (8) balls
Needles: U.S. size 2-3 / 3 mm
Notions: 5 buttons
Gauge: 25 sts and 34 rows in stockinette = 4 x 4 in / 10 x 10 cm.
Adjust needle size to obtain correct gauge if necessary.

SMOCK PATTERN (multiple of 8 + 2 sts)
Row 1 (RS): *P2, insert needle between the 6th and 7th sts as counted from next st, catch yarn, bring through the st and leave on right needle. Knit the first st on left needle and pass the previous st over the new st, k1, p2, k2*; rep * to * and end row with p2.
Rows 2, 3, and 4: Work knit over knit and purl over purl.
Row 5: P2, k2, *p2, insert needle between the 6th and 7th sts as counted from next st, catch yarn, bring through the st and leave on right needle. Knit the first st on left needle and pass the previous st over the new st, k1, p2, k2*; rep * to * and end row with p2, k2, p2.
Rows 6, 7, and 8: Work knit over knit and purl over purl.
Repeat Rows 1-8.

INSTRUCTIONS
BACK
CO 116 (132) sts and knit 8 rows in garter st. Now work in stockinette, always knitting the outermost st at each side as an edge st (edge sts are not included in

pattern). When piece measures 2¾ in /
7 cm, work in smock pattern for 4 in /
10 cm. Work in stockinette again until
piece measures 6¾ (7½) in / 17 (19) cm.

Increase 1 st inside edge st at each side.
Increase the same way every 1¼ in / 3 cm
5 more times = 128 (144) sts. When piece
measures 13¾ (14½) in / 35 (37) cm, shape

armholes: BO 4,1,1 (4,1,1) sts on every other row at each side = 116 (132) sts rem. When armhole measures 3½ (4) / 9 (10) cm, work in smock pattern. When armhole measures 7½ (8¼) in / 19 (21) cm, shape shoulders: BO 15,14,14 (17,17,17) sts on every other row at each side. BO rem 30 (30) sts.

LEFT FRONT

CO 59 (67) sts and knit 8 rows in garter st. Now work in stockinette, always knitting the outermost st at left side as an edge st (the edge st is not included in the pattern) and the last 8 sts at front which are worked in garter st throughout. When piece measures 2¾ in / 7 cm, work in smock pattern for 4 in / 10 cm. Change back to stockinette. When at same length, shape left side as for back = 65 (73) sts. When piece measures 13¾ (14½) in / 35 (37) cm, shape armhole: BO 6,2,2,2,1,1 (6,2,2,2,1,1) sts on every other row = 51 (59) sts rem. When armhole measures 3½ (4) / 9 (10) cm, work in smock pattern. **Note:** The V-neck shaping occurs automatically with the smocking pattern, so no decreases are necessary to shape neckline. When at same length, shape shoulder as for back. Continue working the 8 sts of front band for another 2½ in / 6 cm and then BO. Mark spacing for 5 buttons: Place lowest button approx. 2¾ in / 7 cm from lower edge and top button approx. 2 in / 5 cm below smock pattern at shoulder, with the rest spaced evenly between.

RIGHT FRONT

Work as for left front, reversing shaping. Make buttonholes spaced as for buttons. Make each buttonhole as follows: on RS, k3, BO 3, finish row. On the next row, CO 3 sts over gap.

SLEEVES

CO 52 sts and knit 8 rows in garter st. Now work in stockinette, always knitting the outermost st at each side as an edge st (edge sts are not included in the pattern). When sleeve measures 2 in / 5 cm, work in smock pattern for 3¼ in / 8 cm. Change back to stockinette. When sleeve measures 6¾ in / 17 cm, increase 1 st inside edge st at each side. Increase the same way on every 6th row 11 (15) more times = 76 (84) sts. When sleeve is 17¼ (17¾) in / 44 (45) cm long, begin shaping sleeve cap: BO 5 (5) sts at each side. Now decrease 1 st inside edge st at each side on every other row 14 (17) times and then BO 2 sts at beginning of every row 14 (14) times. BO rem 10 (12) sts. Make the second sleeve the same way.

FINISHING

Read the information about blocking and finishing on page 141 and then block and seam cardigan. Sew front bands around back neck and then seam short ends of bands at center back neck. Sew on buttons.

The sailor cardigan

The marine look is eternally modern, so can a classic sailor sweater ever be wrong? The sailor's collar and its crocheted anchor enhance the marine look and give the cardigan a nostalgic touch invoking the romantic life of the sea. The anchor buttons are another fine detail.

Anna grew up on an island and is drawn to the sea during the summers. She loves vintage—both clothes and beautiful old tools. She is especially enchanted by the charming and colorful outfits of the 1950s.

SIZES: S (M, L)

FINISHED MEASUREMENTS
Length: 22 (22¾, 23¾) in / 56 (58, 60) cm
Chest: 36¼ (38¼, 40¼) in /
92 (97, 102) cm
Sleeve length: 17 (17¼, 17¾) in /
43 (44, 45) cm

MATERIALS
Yarn: CYCA #3 (DK/light worsted),
Garnstudio Drops Karisma Superwash
(109 yd/100 m / 50 g; 100% wool)
Yarn Amounts:
Color 1: Navy Blue #17, 10 (11, 11) balls
Color 2: White #01, 1 (1, 1) balls
Needles: U.S. size 6 / 4 mm
Crochet Hook: U.S. size G-6 / 4 mm
Notions: 5 buttons; stitch holder
Gauge: 21 sts and 28 rows in stockinette =
4 x 4 in / 10 x 10 cm.
Adjust needle size to obtain correct gauge
if necessary.

SEED STITCH
Row 1: *K1, p1*; rep * to * across.
Row 2: Work purl over knit and knit over purl.
Repeat Row 2.

INSTRUCTIONS
BACK
With Color 1, CO 94 (100, 106) sts and work in stockinette for 1¼ in / 3 cm. Knit 1 row on WS for foldline and then work another 1¼ in / 3 cm in stockinette, always knitting the outermost st at each side as an edge st. Now work in color stripe sequence as follows: 4 rows Color 2, 2 rows Color 1, 4 rows Color 2 and then continue with Color 1 only. When piece measures 14½ (15, 15½) in / 37 (38, 39) cm from the fold-line, shape armhole: BO 3,1,1,1 (3,2,1,1; 3,2,2,1) sts at each side on every other row = 82 (86, 90) sts rem. When armhole measures 7½ (8, 8¼) in / 19 (20, 21) cm, BO the center 12 (12, 12) sts for back neck

and work each side separately. At neck edge, BO another 6 sts on every other row 2 times = 23 (25, 27) sts. *At the same time* as shaping neckline, shape shoulder: BO 8,8,7 (9,8,8; 9,9,9) sts on every other row. Work the other side the same way, reversing shaping.

LEFT FRONT
With Color 1, CO 53 (57, 61) sts and work in stockinette for 1¼ in / 3 cm. Knit 1 row on WS for foldline. Place the outermost 7 sts at front edge on a holder and then work another 1¼ in / 3 cm in stockinette, always knitting the outermost st at left side as an edge st. When at same length, work the stripes and shape armhole as for back = 40 (43, 46) sts rem. *At the same time* as the first bind-off for the armhole, begin shaping neckline: on RS, k2tog inside edge st. Decrease the same way on, alternately, every other and every 4th row 16 (17, 18) more times. When at same length, shape shoulder as for back.

RIGHT FRONT
Work as for left front, reversing shaping.

SLEEVES
With Color 1, CO 42 (44, 46) sts and work in stockinette for 1¼ in / 3 cm. Knit 1 row on WS for foldline and then continue in stockinette, always knitting the outermost st at each side as an edge st. When at same length, work color stripes as for back and front. When piece measures 2 (2½, 2¾) in / 5 (6, 7) cm from foldline, increase 1 st inside edge st at each side. Increase the same way every ¾ in / 2 cm 16 (17, 18) times = 76 (80, 84) sts. When sleeve is 17 (17¼, 17¾) in / 43 (44, 45) cm from the foldline, shape sleeve cap: BO 3 sts at each side and then decrease 1 st inside edge st at each side on every RS row 12 (13, 14) times. Next, BO 2 sts at beginning of every row 6 (6, 6) times and, finally, BO 3 sts at beginning of every row 8 (8, 8) times. BO rem 10 (12, 14) sts. Make another sleeve the same way.

FRONT BANDS
For the left front band: Pick up the 7 sts on holder and work in garter st until the band reaches the base of V-neck. BO. Mark spacing for 5 buttons along front band: Place lowest button 2¾ in / 7 cm above foldline and top button ⅜ in / 1 cm below base of V-neck, with the rest spaced evenly between.

For the right front band: Work as for left front band but make buttonholes spaced as for buttons. Make each buttonhole on RS as follows: K2, BO 2, k3. On the next row, CO 2 sts over the gap.

FINISHING
Read the information about blocking and finishing on page 141 and then block and seam cardigan. Make a slit at each side by beginning side seam 2 in / 5 cm above

foldline. Fold under all the facings and sew down on WS. Sew on buttons.

SAILOR'S COLLAR

With Color 1, CO 84 (86, 88) sts and work in seed st for 4 rows. Change to stockinette except for the 4 outermost sts at each side that continue in seed st throughout. When collar is 8 (8¼, 8¾) in / 20 (21, 22) cm long, BO the center 12 (12, 12) sts and work each side separately. Shape neck: BO 6 sts on every other row 2 times. Now begin shaping one side of collar: On RS, k2tog inside the seed st edging on every other row 17 (18, 19) times. Work 4 (4, 6) rows and then BO rem 7 (7, 7) sts. Work the other side of the collar the same way, reversing shaping.

DECORATIVE BAND

With Color 2, CO 5 sts and work as follows: K1 (edge st), 3 sts stockinette, k1 (edge st). Continue as set until band measures approx. 48¾ (49¼, 50) in / 124 (125, 127) cm—the band should be long enough to fit around the collar. BO. Sew the band inside the seed st edging of the collar. Sew the collar around neck and short ends of front bands.

ANCHOR

With Color 2, ch 20 and join into a ring with 1 sl st to 1st ch. Work 20 sc around ring and end with 1 sl st into 1st sc. Ch 20 new sts, skip 1 ch and work back with 17 sc towards the ring. Ch 5 new sts, skip the 1st ch and work 4 sc back (towards ring). Work 1 sl st into next ch and 1 sc in the last ch just before the ring, 1 sl st into ring. Cut yarn.

Continue as follows: Work 1 sc on the opposite side of the same ch where the last sc was worked (just below the ring). Ch 5 new sts, skip the 1st ch and work back (towards ring), work 1 sl st and then 17 sc on the opposite side of the previously worked 17 sc. Cut yarn.

Now work as: Ch 26, insert hook in the 2nd ch from the hook and work 23 sc, and then 5 sc in the last ch, sc 23 on the opposite side of the newly worked 23 sc and end with 5 sc in the last ch. Cut yarn.

Center the anchor on the collar and sew on securely: Begin with the ring and then sew down the rest of the anchor. Arch up both ends and sew them down well.

The skater's cardigan

A sweater with a hood is especially nice. This cardigan is easy to knit and the block pattern makes a textured and almost cable-like surface. The warm hood gets a pretty lift from some glamorous fake fur or swan's down edgings.

Team or synchronized skating is a branch of ice skating where the team moves together harmoniously and in formation in step with the music. Team Boomerang consists of about 20 members and on a number of occasions has placed well in international competitions.

SIZES: S (M, L)

FINISHED MEASUREMENTS
Length: 21¾ (22½, 23¼) in /
55 (57, 59) cm
Chest: 37½ (39½, 41¼) in /
95 (100, 105) cm
Sleeve length: 16½ (17, 17¼) in /
42 (43, 44) cm

MATERIALS
Yarn: CYCA #4 (afghan/aran/worsted),
Rowan Alpaca Cotton (148 yd/135 m / 50
g; 72% alpaca, 28% cotton)
Yarn Amounts: Raindrop #404, 8 (8, 9)
balls
Needles: U.S. size 8 / 5 mm
Notions: separating zipper, 18-20 in / 45-
50 cm long; tie cord for the hood, approx.
47¼ in / 120 cm; swan's down or fake fur
band, approx. 31½ in / 80 cm
Gauge: 16 sts and 22 rows in stockinette =
4 x 4 in / 10 x 10 cm.

Adjust needle size to obtain correct gauge
if necessary.

BLOCK PATTERN (multiple of 6 + 2 sts)
Row 1 (RS): Knit.
Row 2 (WS): Purl.
Row 3: *K2, p4*; rep * to * across, ending
with k2.
Rows 4, 5, and 6: Work purl over purl and
knit over knit.
Row 7: Knit.
Row 8: Purl.
Row 9: P3, *k2, p4*; rep * to * across, end-
ing with k2, p3.
Rows 10, 11, and 12: Work purl over purl
and knit over knit.
Repeat Rows 1-12.

INSTRUCTIONS
BACK
CO 76 (82, 88) sts and work in stockinette
for ¾ in / 2 cm. Knit 1 row on WS (foldline). Begin block pattern, always knitting

the outermost st at each side as an edge st (edge sts are not included in the pattern). When piece measures 13¾ (14¼, 14½) in / 35 (36, 37) cm from foldline, begin shaping armholes: BO 2 sts at each side. Now

begin raglan shaping: K1, k2tog, work in pattern to last 3 sts, ssk, k1. Decrease the same way on every other row 27 (28, 29) more times. Work 1 row and then BO rem 16 (20, 24) sts.

LEFT FRONT

CO 40 (43, 46) sts and work in stockinette for ¾ in / 2 cm. Knit 1 row on WS (foldline). Begin block pattern, always knitting the outermost st at each side as an edge st (edge sts are not included in the pattern). **Note:** On size M, Row 3 ends with k2, p3 and Row 9 ends with k2. Otherwise, work the pattern as above.

When piece measures 13¾ (14¼, 14½) in / 35 (36, 37) cm from foldline, begin shaping armhole: BO 2 sts at left side. Now begin raglan shaping as for back on every other row at left side a total of 24 (25, 26) times.

Note: There are 4 fewer raglan decreases (= 8 fewer rows) on the front than on the back.

At the same time as the 15th (16th, 17th) decrease, BO 5,2,2,1,1 (5,2,2,2,1; 5,2,2,2,2) sts on every other row for neck. When 3 (4, 5) sts rem, work 1 more row and then BO rem sts.

RIGHT FRONT

Work as for left front, reversing shaping.

SLEEVES

CO 40 sts and work in stockinette for ¾ in / 2 cm. Knit 1 row on WS (foldline). Begin block pattern, always knitting the outermost st at each side as an edge st (edge sts are not included in the pattern). When sleeve is 1½ in / 4 cm above foldline, increase 1 st inside edge st at each side. Increase the same way every ¾ in / 2 cm 8

(9, 10) more times = 58 (60, 62) sts. Work new sts into pattern. When sleeve is 16½ (17, 17¼) in / 42 (43, 44) cm from foldline, shape sleeve cap: BO 2 sts at each side. Now shape raglan as for back a total of 26 (27, 28) times.

Note: There are 2 fewer raglan decreases (= 4 fewer rows) on the sleeves than on the back.

When 2 sts rem, work 1 rows and then BO. Make the second sleeve the same way.

HOOD

CO 118 (124, 130) sts and work in stockinette for ¾ in / 2 cm. Knit 1 row on WS (foldline). Begin block pattern, always knitting the outermost st at each side as an edge st (edge sts are not included in the pattern). When piece measures 9½ (9¾, 10¼) in / 24 (25, 26) cm from foldline, BO all sts.

FINISHING

Read the information about blocking and finishing on page 141 and then block and seam cardigan. Turn in all the facings and sew down on WS. Sew in zipper down center front. Fold the hood at the center, with RS facing RS and sew down the sides that do not have facings. Fold in the front edge along foldline and sew down on WS so that a casing is formed. Sew the hood securely around the neck. Thread the tie cord through the casing. Sew the swan's down or fake fur along the hood opening and on the ends of the tie cord.

The theater cardigan

A lovely cardigan that is quick to knit and will warm your knees as you work. Heavy yarn, big needles, and a simple pattern combine for success.

Susanna works as a theater producer and is the spider at the center of the web in her workplace. She is constantly running up the stairs and down the passages and often goes all out to solve the many large and small problems that can occur in a theater with several parallel performances in its schedule.

SIZES: S (M, L)

FINISHED MEASUREMENTS
Length: 26½ (27¼, 28) in / 67 (69, 71) cm
Chest: 35½ (37½, 39½) in / 90 (95, 100) cm
Sleeve length: 17¾ (18¼, 18½) in / 45 (46, 47) cm

MATERIALS
Yarn: CYCA #6, Rowan Drift (87 yd/80 m / 100 g; 100% Merino wool)
Yarn Amounts: Solo 910, 9 (10, 11) balls
Needles: U.S. size 15 / 9 mm
Notions: 5 buttons; stitch holder
Gauge: 11 sts and 16 rows in pattern = 4 x 4 in / 10 x 10 cm.
Adjust needle size to obtain correct gauge if necessary.

PATTERN (multiple of 3 + 2 sts)
Row 1 (RS): K2, *sl 1 wyb, k2*; rep * to * across.

Row 2: K2, *p1, k2*; rep * to * across.
Repeat Rows 1-2.

INSTRUCTIONS
BACK
CO 49 (52, 55) sts and purl 1 row. Now work in pattern, always knitting the outermost st at each side as an edge st (edge sts are not included in the pattern). When piece measures 19 (19¼, 19¾) in / 48 (49, 50) cm, shape armholes: BO 2,1,1,1 sts at each side = 39 (42, 45) sts rem. When armhole measures 7½ (8, 8¼) in / 19 (20, 21) cm, BO the center 9 (10, 11) sts for back neck and then work each side separately. Shape shoulder: on every other row, BO 8,7 (8,8; 9,8) sts. Work the other side the same way, reversing shaping.

LEFT FRONT
CO 29 (32, 35) sts and purl 1 row. Now work in pattern, always knitting the outermost st at left side as an edge st (edge sts

are not included in the pattern) and the 5 sts at center front edge which are knitted on all rows for front band. When piece measures 5¼ in / 13 cm, make pocket opening: On RS, work 9 (9, 9) sts, BO the next 10 sts; place rem sts on a holder. Make the pocket lining: CO 10 sts and work in stockinette for 4¼ in / 11 cm. Place these sts over the 10 sts bound off for pocket opening and complete row. Continue in pattern. When at same length, shape armhole: On every other row at side, BO 2,1,1 sts = 25 (28, 31) sts. When armhole measures 4 (4¼, 4¾) in / 10 (11, 12) cm, BO 6 (7, 8) sts at front edge for neck. Next, at neck edge, on every other row, decrease 1 st 4 (5, 6) times = 15 (16, 17) sts rem. When at same length, shape shoulder as for back.

Mark spacing for 5 buttons along front band: Place lowest button approx. 4 in / 10 cm above lower edge and top button approx. ¾ in / 2 cm below short end of front band, with the rest spaced evenly between.

RIGHT FRONT

Work as for left front, reversing shaping. **Note:** Set up pattern with the slipped st nearest the 5 knit sts of front band so that left and right fronts will be mirror image. For buttonholes, work on RS, spacing as for buttons. For each buttonhole: k2, BO 2 sts, complete row. On the next row, CO 2 sts over gap.

SLEEVES

CO 25 sts and purl 1 row. Now work in pattern, always knitting the outermost st at each side as an edge st (edge sts are not included in the pattern). When sleeve measures 4 in / 10 cm, increase 1 st inside edge st at each side. Increase the same way every 1½ in / 4 cm 6 (7, 8) more times = 39 (41, 43) sts; work new sts into pattern. When sleeve measures 17¾ (18¼, 18½) in / 45 (46, 47) cm, begin shaping sleeve cap: BO 2 sts at each side. Now decrease 1 st at each side on every other row 6 (7, 8) times and then BO 2 sts at beginning of every row 8 (8, 8) times. BO rem 7 (7, 7) sts. Make the second sleeve the same way.

FINISHING

Read the information about blocking and finishing on page 141 and then block and seam cardigan, leaving 4 in / 10 cm open at lower edge of sides for a slit. Sew down pocket linings on WS. Sew on buttons.

COLLAR

CO 11 sts and purl 1 row. Work in pattern for approx. 19¾ in / 50 cm and then BO across. Sew collar securely along neck edge.

POCKET FLAPS

CO 8 sts and purl 1 row. Work in pattern for approx. 5½ in / 14 cm and then BO across. Make a second pocket flap the same way. Securely sew on flaps above pocket openings.

The Christmas cardigan

This graphic pattern is really fun to knit. It can look like blocks or flowers, depending on how you choose to regard it. The wavy pattern of the long sleeve cuffs will beautifully warm your frozen wrists.

On Christmas Eve morning, Maria is up early to make sure that all the last minute Christmas preparations are ready before she wakes the rest of the family with a traditional Christmas breakfast. She inherited her fine nightgown from her grandmother as well as the pretty, antique Christmas ornaments that are lovingly taken out of the old boxes every year.

SIZES: S-M (M-L)

FINISHED MEASUREMENTS
Length: 17¼ (18½) in / 44 (47) cm
Chest: 37½ (41¼) in / 95 (105) cm
Sleeve length: 18½ (19¼) in / 47 (49) cm

MATERIALS
Yarn: CYCA #4 (afghan/aran/worsted), Garnstudio Drops Alaska (76 yd/69 m / 50 g; 100% wool)
Yarn Amounts:
Color 1: Dark Red #11, 8 (9) balls
Color 2: Off White #02, 6 (6) balls
Needles: U.S. size 6 / 4 mm
Notions: 6 buttons; stitch holder
Gauge: 17 sts and 22 rows in pattern = 4 x 4 in / 10 x 10 cm.
Adjust needle size to obtain correct gauge if necessary.

PATTERN FOR SLEEVE CUFFS (multiple of 11 sts)
Row 1 (WS): Purl.
Row 2: Knit.
Row 3: Purl.
Row 4: *K2tog, k3, yo, k1, yo, k3, k2tog*; rep * to * across.
Rows 5, 7, 9, 11, and 13: Purl.
Rows 6, 8, 10, and 12: Work as for Row 4.
Rows 14 and 15: Knit.
Row 16: Purl.
Row 17: Knit.
Repeat Rows 4-17.

INSTRUCTIONS
BACK
With Color 1, CO 82 (92) sts and work in stockinette for 1¼ in / 3 cm. Knit 1 row on WS (foldline) and then knit 4 rows in garter st. Change to stockinette, and, *at the same time,* decrease 8 (10) sts evenly spaced

on the 2nd stockinette row = 74 (82) sts rem. Change to Color 2, work 2 rows in stockinette and then work following the chart, always knitting the outermost st at each side as an edge st. Work 4 (5) pattern repeats between the edge sts.

Note: On size S-M, work 4 sts with Color 2 between the edge st and pattern repeats on both sides so that the pattern will be centered on the back.

When piece measures 2 in / 5 cm from the foldline, increase 1 st inside the edge st at each side. Increase the same way every 1½ in / 4 cm 3 more times = 82 (90) sts. Work the new sts with Color 2. When piece measures 9¾ (10¼) in / 25 (26) cm, shape armhole: BO 3,2,1,1,1,1 (3,2,2,1,1,1) sts on every other row at each side = 64 (70) sts rem.

Work a total of 5 pattern repeats in length and end with 2 rows with Color 2. Work the rest of the back with Color 1. When armhole measures 7½ (8¼) in / 19 (21) cm, BO the center 18 (20) sts for back neck.

Work each side separately.
Shape shoulder: BO 7,6,6 (7,7,7) sts on every other row and, *at the same time,* BO 2 sts on every other row at neck edge 2 times. Work the other side the same way, reversing shaping.

LEFT FRONT
With Color 1, CO 47 (52) sts and work in stockinette for 1¼ in / 3 cm. Knit 1 row on WS (foldline). Place the outermost 6 sts at front edge on a holder. Knit 4 rows in garter st. Change to stockinette and, on the 2nd row, decrease 4 (5) sts evenly spaced across = 37 (41) sts rem. Change to Color 2 and work 2 rows in stockinette. Now work following the chart, always knitting the outermost st at left side as an edge st. Work 2 (2½) pattern repeats across inside edge sts (the half repeat in size M-L should be placed at center front).
Note: On size S-M, work 4 sts with Color 2 between the edge st and the pattern repeats on the left side to that the pattern will be placed correctly at the front edge. When at same length, increase at side and bind off for armhole as for back = 32 (35) sts rem. When armhole measures 6¼ (6¾) in / 16 (17) cm, BO 5,2,2,2,2 (6,2,2,2,2) sts on every other row at neck edge. When at same length, shape shoulder as for back.

RIGHT FRONT
Work as for left front, reversing shaping.

SLEEVES
With Color 1, CO 57 (57) sts and work in pattern for sleeve cuffs, always knitting the outermost st at each side as an edge st. Repeat the pattern 2 times = 31 rows. Change to Color 2, work 2 rows in stockinette, decreasing 7 (7) sts evenly spaced inside edge sts on the 1st row of stockinette = 50 (50) sts rem. Now work following the chart, with the pattern inside the edge sts. When sleeve measures 13 (16) cm, increase 1 st inside edge st at each side. Increase the same way every 1¼ in / 3 cm 5 (7) more times = 62 (66) sts. Work new sts into pattern.
When sleeve is 18½ (19¼) in / 47 (49) cm long, shape sleeve cap: BO 3 sts at each side. Now decrease 1 st inside edge st at each side on every other row 13 (14) times and then BO 2 sts at beginning of every row 8 (8) times. BO rem 14 (16) sts. Make the second sleeve the same way.

FRONT BANDS
Pick up the 6 sts set aside on left front and, with Color 1, work in k1, p1 ribbing except for the last st next to front edge (to be used for seaming) which is always knitted as an edge st. Continue in ribbing until band, when slightly stretched, reaches neckline. BO.
Mark spacing for 6 buttons along band: Place lowest button 1½ in / 4 cm from lower edge and top button ⅜ in / 1 cm from neckline, with the rest spaced evenly between.

Work the right front band as for left band but make buttonholes spaced as for buttons. For each buttonhole: On RS, rib 2 sts, BO 2 sts, rib 2 sts. On the next row, CO 2 sts over the gap.

FINISHING

Read the information about blocking and finishing on page 141 and then block and seam cardigan. Turn facings in and sew down on WS. Sew on buttons.

NECKBAND

Begin and end neckband inside front bands. With Color 1, pick up and knit approx. 55 (60) sts along neck. Work in stockinette for ¾ in / 2 cm. Change to Color 2 and knit 1 row on WS (foldline). Work in stockinette for ¾ in / 2 cm. BO all sts. Turn in neckband at foldline and sew down on WS.

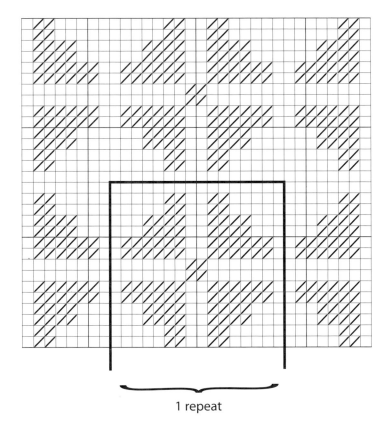

◪ = dark red

☐ = off white

1 repeat

ABBREVIATIONS

BO	bind off (British: cast off)
ch	chain
cm	centimeter(s)
CO	cast on
dc	double crochet (= British treble crochet)
in	inch(es)
k	knit
k2tog	knit 2 together (right-leaning decrease)
m	meter(s)
mm	millimeter(s)
p	purl
rem	remain(s)(ing)
rep	repeat(s)
rnd(s)	round(s)
RS	right side
sc	single crochet (= British double crochet)
sl	slip
ssk	(slip one knitwise) 2 times, insert left needle into back of the 2 sts and knit together through back loops (left-leaning decrease; substitutes for sl 1, k1, psso)
st(s)	stitch(es)
stockinette	= British stocking st
t-ch	turning chain
WS	wrong side
wyb	with yarn held in back
wyf	with yarn held in front
yd	yard(s)

Tips from the author

Always begin any knitting or crochet project with a gauge swatch. That way you can be sure that you are using the right needle or crochet hook size and that the final result will have the dimensions as intended in the pattern. Here's how to make a gauge swatch:

Knit or crochet a swatch that is 4 x 4 in / 10 x 10 cm using the needles or hook recommended in the instructions. Next, count the number of stitches and rows and compare your swatch with the recommended gauge. If there are more stitches than specified in the instructions, change to a slightly larger size needle or hook. If there are fewer stitches, try a smaller size needle or hook.

You don't have to use the yarn suggested in the pattern but if you substitute another yarn—or even a totally different type of yarn—it is especially important to make a gauge swatch because different types of yarn produce different gauges.

If you are working a pattern with several colors, you might want to wind a small ball of each color. That makes it easier to keep the strands separate as you work and avoid unnecessary tangling.

The best thing about making your own cardigan—apart from the satisfaction of creating something pretty with your own hands—is that you can fit the sweater to your own measurements and desires. If, for example, you want to lengthen a sweater—no problem! Just measure and follow your own measurements.

Bind off all pieces loosely and allow some extra time for finishing and sewing your cardigan together. First, dampen all the pieces a little by spraying water on the pieces and then pressing them lightly with a steam iron so that they will assume the correct shape and so that any edges rolling in will be smoothed out. However, before you iron the cardigan, read the information on the yarn ball band. Some yarns such as synthetics, angora, and other long-haired fibers should not be pressed. Also take extra care with cotton yarn because cotton is not as elastic and can lose its shape if ironed too hard.

Let the pieces dry completely before sewing the cardigan together. It is best to seam the sweater with the same yarn that you knitted or crocheted with. You can use the extra yarn from the cast-on tail or ends left from cutting the skein. That helps you avoid having too many ends to weave in.

It is smart to save the yarn ball band with the garment care instructions so that you will know how to wash and care for the garment in the best way.

Last but not least: Give yourself a lot of time to create, enjoy your handwork, and avoid stressing when you are knitting or crocheting. Part of the charm is the time you have to sit still and see how the work develops. As your reward, you'll have a unique cardigan that is well-made and will keep you warm for a long time.

Yarn Information

YARN SUPPLIERS
Nordic Mart Inc.
U.S. Drops Superstore
1229 A Carmel Street
San Luis Obispo, CA 93401
www.nordicmart.com

Westminster Fibers (US)
8 Shelter Drive
Greer, SC 29650
info@westminsterfibers.com
www.westminsterfibers.com

Webs – America's Yarn Store
75 Service Center Road
Northampton, MA 01060
800-367-9327
www.yarn.com
customerservice@yarn.com

If you are unable to obtain any of the yarn used in this book, it can be replaced with a yarn of a similar weight and composition. Please note, however, the finished projects may vary slightly from those shown, depending on the yarn used.

For more information on selecting or substituting yarn contact your local yarn shop or an online store, they are familiar with all types of yarns and would be happy to help you. Additionally, the online knitting community at Ravelry.com has forums where you can post questions about specific yarns. Yarns come and go so quickly these days and there are so many beautiful yarns available.

Acknowledgments

My warmest thanks to:
Our wonderful team: the fantastic photographer Åsa Dahlgren for transforming my dreams and always taking the most wonderful pictures. The super creative stylist Gudrun Bonér, whose magic wand creates the luscious environments and who brings out all the accessories from her treasure chest to make the photos lovely. The hair and make-up artist Regina Törnvall who with her empathy, sensitive ear, and brushes and pencils can change anyone into a super model.

Dina Cedervret and Marianne Jansson who, on short notice and with a huge degree of professionalism, substituted for Regina when she had to travel to the other side of the globe for another job.

All the models, who were my sources for inspiration and who so kindly shared their

passions, their lives, and their time. You gave each cardigan a soul.

My great family: Niklas, Axel, and Greta, who put up with all my knitting, who always supported me, and who made me happy every day!

A big thank you to:
Bibbi Blomqvist, Eva Wincent, Anne Hallberg, Martina Andersson and Gunnar Björling, Yvonne Larsson and Broström's Association, The Palm House in Göteborg, the Wind Wagon Project, Floramor and Kruka-tös, Café Rosteriet Da Matteo in Göteborg, Ami Lanmark's Studio, the Vicarage 101 in Slöinge, Barken Viking, Dance Forum, Frölundaborg, The Botanical Gardens in Göteborg, Backa Theater, Delfins Summer home organization Stora Förö, Second Saddle, Pace Jeans, and everyone else who contributed to making this book possible.